Go...g

Good Practice in Psychotherapy and Counselling

The Exceptional Relationship

DON FEASEY MA

Psychoanalytic Psychotherapist

W

WHURR PUBLISHERS

LONDON AND PHILADELPHIA

© 2000 Whurr Publishers
First published 2000 by
Whurr Publishers Ltd
19b Compton Terrace, London N1 2UN, England, and
325 Chestnut Street, Philadelphia PA 19106, USA

British Library Cataloguing in Publication Data
A catalogue record for this book is available from the
British Library.

ISBN 1 86156 144 X

Printed and bound in the UK by Athenaeum Press Ltd,
Gateshead, Tyne & Wear

Contents

Dedication

Thanks to Jeanne who, some twenty years ago, drew my attention to psychotherapy as a possible profession.

Thanks to Jane, Simon, Jon and Tim who have always tried to understand and support my choice.

Thanks to Gerald, Martin, Eric and Tony who got me started.

Thanks to Dean and Doreen who never failed to encourage me.

Thanks to Barbara and Keith who helped to make it possible, and to all my present and former clients, without exception.

Introduction

This book arose out of a lecture I gave some years ago to a gathering of colleagues meeting in a psychotherapy interest group. Members give talks and run workshops for the mutual benefit of the membership of the group. I volunteered to give a talk in which I would set out the problems and advantages of running a private practice in psychotherapy, the practice being run from my own home in a small city in the North West of England. At the time of giving this talk I was also employed on a sessional basis as a principal psychotherapist with a large urban health authority based in a day therapeutic community. Most of the people I was addressing worked either in the National Health Service or Social Services, though there were one or two independent counsellors and therapists present. In all about thirty people were present at the lecture. I can only say that my talk was met with a certain coolness. There was at that time a certain hostility to what I was doing — especially from those who identified me with psychoanalysis. This was because I was in private practice. For some health workers present there was an odium surrounding the phrase 'private practice' and what was implied by it. It should be remembered that I am talking about the NHS some twenty years ago and psychotherapy barely existed outside London and perhaps Edinburgh. The world of counselling also barely existed and the work of Carl Rogers, that distinguished thinker and practitioner in psychotherapy, was only acknowledged in very limited quarters. The fantasy of analytic psychotherapy, which had currency at the time, was of heavily Viennese-accented middle-aged men charging absurdly high private fees for analysis to mostly highly neurotic 'spoilt' ladies, with questionable benefit other than to the analyst's bank balance. Now many years later that image is somewhat dulled but prejudice still exists. However, there have been big changes: psychotherapy and counselling are now on the scene and it is those changes that I wished to address in the process of writing this book. The book is intended for readers who are substantially, but not exclusively, working as independent practitioners — mainly in private practice — or are contemplating doing so. Many therapists and counsellors work in both the public and private sector and I hope some of the issues I address will take into account the institutional context in which they sometimes operate.

In the North West of England and throughout the British Isles there has arisen a steady demand for a 'talking psychotherapy' and this not just in the alternative and fringe therapeutic cultures of therapists outside mainstream psychiatric medicine. The demand has come from both non-patients and patients who, with some experience of traditional drug-based therapy, have grown impatient with the limitations of that therapy and see that there is advantage and real gain to be enjoyed through the realms of psychotherapy and counselling, where feelings are taken seriously and patients are encouraged to take responsibility for their own health.

There has been a positive response from the NHS, both within its hospital settings and especially within the General Practice services. Alongside this quickening of interest and the resulting quest for training by health professionals has come a need for a theory and methodology of therapy and counselling that can be employed in a treatment and training process.

And so psychoanalysis has been discovered again; after years of neglect and denigration Sigmund Freud has been found to have had something to say about the human psyche in all its manifestations of individual, family and social life. The unconscious has been discovered — again! Modern interpreters of psychoanalysis now abound and a whole new world of counselling psychology is coming into being based on the work of Carl Rogers, whose work is now generally accepted and celebrated. Although there is much competitive rivalry and the debate is often fractious and hard to take seriously, nevertheless the outcome has been productive in what is now on offer to patients: worried and disturbed people in a worried and disturbed world.

Another important spin-off from this rapid development of interest in psychoanalytic psychotherapy has been the growth of private practice. Most psychotherapy practitioners in the NHS have received therapy themselves from independent private psychotherapists as part of their own training. Virtually all counsellors are trained in experiential self-development groups. Indeed the first principle of therapy and counselling is often defined as seeing the therapist as the most experienced patient. To preserve confidentiality and autonomy the trainee analytic psychotherapist is actively encouraged to find 'training treatment' in the private sector. Many counsellors engage in a counselling relationship for their own benefit. Private supervision is now commonly available to both psychotherapists and counsellors. As a result of this the traditional antagonism towards both private practice and an analytical/counselling approach to mental health has been moderated in a benign direction — at least in some quarters! There is still much to be achieved.

Traditional psychiatric medicine still tends to regard psychotherapy with much scepticism and the world of clinical psychology is only now beginning to take a real interest, abandoning with reluctance its attachment to so called scientific enquiry and practice. Cognitive analytic therapy seems very attractive to many psychologists, so change is taking place and this book is a response to change. Independent private practice in psychotherapy and counselling is becoming a reality throughout Britain. Its presence is still patchy and the United Kingdom Council for Psychotherapy handbook is at present rather misleading in its listing of psychotherapists throughout the country. Many of them are available only through the health service and are not very easily reached through the usual referral channels. The British Association for Counselling provides another register showing 'qualified' full members of the Association and those who, for the most part, are still in training. Waiting lists in the public sector are anything up to two years. Therapy or counselling may also, where provided, be severely time limited; this is especially true of the GP practice provision. Therapy is no longer being seen as the privilege of a wealthy few. More and more 'ordinary' people of relatively modest means are seeking it as a right and faced with a shortage of service in the NHS are going out into the market looking for competent, properly trained and regulated practitioners.

Analytic psychotherapy has a mixed background stretching back some hundred years. It has been attacked and de-bunked by scientific psychology and medicine, including psychiatry; it has been abused by practitioners who have been ill informed and messianic in their claims on its behalf; it has been isolated by cliques of analysts who have tried to hold on to it as if it were capable of being possessed like a piece of property. The history of counselling is less fraught and its growing presence in GP practice services and clinical psychology departments is evidence of its current health. Nevertheless there has been a proliferation of counselling courses on offer in further education colleges, some of which have been quite inadequate in preparing student counsellors for further training and practice. The atmosphere is changing and a new phase of development and progress is opening up, to the benefit of potential clients and therapy/counsellor trainees. The United Kingdom Council for Psychotherapy, together with the British Association for Counselling Register, is the most obvious institutional evidence of this change and I hope, too, this book will play its modest part in that movement.

As well as to independent practitioners this book is addressed to the needs of trainees in psychotherapy and counselling. It should not be forgotten that Carl Rogers described himself as a psychotherapist, practising client-centred psychotherapy; it is with respect to his position that I place psychotherapist and counsellor together in a common practical framework of reference. The book is intended to provide an understanding of the framework of the therapeutic relationship and it attempts to do so without deferring to any particular theoretical orientation. Having said that, I know I will stir up some protests from both camps. Strong theoretical and cultural differences threaten to keep the analytical and counselling schools at a distance from each other; sometimes, regrettably, in opposition. The framework of much psychoanalytic work is often described in terms of gender or non-gender issues which may, or may not, be very real or pertinent. As Stephen Frosh writes in his book *Sexual Difference: Masculinity and Psychoanalysis*, '[gender] a subject which will not go away', and he argues that 'psychoanalysis, at its very core, is about sexual differences'. Many counsellors would look for a different central concern. In this book I do not attempt to reconcile any theory or position, rather the approach is practical so the chapters are organized around such topics as time, place, referrals, appointments, money, the world beyond the consulting room, communications and professionalism. Other authors refer to this conceptualization as the frame of therapy (Gray, 1994).

I have used case material in the form of vignettes to illustrate this book and I hope readers will gain benefit from the experience of my clients, in the NHS and in my private practice, from my group practice and from my couples, family and individual practice. In all cases I have changed the names, places and times of the encounters described and in some cases changed the gender of the subjects in the service of anonymity and confidentiality. I will discuss this latter issue at greater length in the book.

I am indebted to my past and present clients and wish to pay tribute and offer thanks to them for their assistance in a mutual learning process.

Finally, I hope this book will encourage rather than discourage those starting the journey into the world of counselling and psychotherapy and make their journey a little easier.

Don Feasey

Chapter 1
Beginnings

Ends and Beginnings — there are no such things/ There are only Middles.
(Robert Frost in *The Home Stretch*. Jonathon Cape)

The reader should remember that although psychotherapy, from the analytic tradition, has been present in the UK since the 1930s it has only within the last twenty years begun cautiously to impinge on the lives of the majority of the clinical population of the mentally and emotionally distressed. For historical reasons, psychoanalysis, in its fragmented representation in London in the postwar period, failed to gain any significant foothold in psychiatry or clinical psychology. On the contrary, 'new' electric shock, chemical treatments and behavioural management ruled the roost for a very long time. Formal academic psychology teaching in the universities moved away from analytical ideas towards either a more humanistic, developmental model, or to a preoccupation with behaviour and measurement.

The insularity of the psychoanalytic movement in London did nothing to encourage any challenge to these practices. With the honourable exception of the Tavistock Clinic and one or two other specialist centres of treatment or education, psychoanalytic method and theory were held jealously in the possession of a very few 'pure' private analysts and institutes in London. For years any attempt by individuals to challenge that hegemony was doomed to failure. This condition was perpetuated too by the hostility of the great majority of psychiatrists and psychologists to analytical ideas. The atmosphere of animosity and ridicule exhibited towards psychoanalytic theory in the universities was most marked. It undermined the free exchange of ideas and experience. Teachers like myself, interested in psychoanalytic ideas, were treated with suspicion and scorn. Only in the humanities was psychoanalysis treated as a historical experience of interest, especially in relation to the study of literature. An earlier period of genuine and sympathetic interest had gone and the new schools of psychology, with their emphasis on objectivity, behaviourism and ratio-

5

nality, had no room to admit to there being any relevance in the psychology of subjectivity and emotionality.

However, there was a growing discontent among the *consumers* of psychiatry and psychology and a number of radical psychiatrists were beginning to express their deep discontent with chemical management of patients. Outstanding among them was R.D. Laing (1960), and his book *The Divided Self* resonated among the many young doctors, psychologists and therapists working in mental health. Gradually this movement fed through into the culture of medicine and the various theories of human relationships being taught in schools, colleges and universities. Radicalism was in the air and psychiatry and clinical psychology came under critical scrutiny. An anti-psychiatry movement found its voice, demanding that patients suffering emotional and mental disturbance should be given a say in their treatment and that attention be drawn toward their essentially human needs for understanding with compassion and dignity. As a result new ideas, often based on earlier radical theories, came to the fore. Psychoanalysis itself came in for a more radical, critical appraisal and alternative therapeutic theories were proposed that demanded serious attention. Discussion on subjects such as gender and race, sexuality and class were the order of the day and the dominance of the professional clinical practitioners of the time was called into question.

This was the background to my own pursuit of a new start in my professional life as a psychotherapist. I had been for some twenty years a lecturer in higher education concerned with training youth and community workers and schoolteachers. A thread of interest for me, throughout, had been concern with the working of the conscious and unconscious mind. Fate then took a hand. In 1978 a crisis was developing in vocational higher education. The part of it I was then concerned with, the education and training of secondary school teachers, was threatened with enormous cutbacks and, with it, a matching loss of jobs in the area of professional training.

For some of my colleagues this was tantamount to professional disaster but for me it was an opportunity. I was 49 years old. I had enough time ahead to think of another career or at least an occupation. The problem was, how to do it?

At about the age of 16 I encountered girls and the work of Sigmund Freud (1900). Confronting my sexuality in a completely immature, half comprehending way I read every Freud text I could lay my hands upon. Thank heavens for the inter-library loan service in the UK! After Freud came D.H. Lawrence. Paradoxically I found Marx at about the same time and lapped him up too. Somehow I resolved the contradictions inherent in these supposedly opposing ideologies.

I became a youth worker and teacher and eventually a trainer of teachers and youth workers. Within the College of Education where I worked, students had been talking enthusiastically about Carl Rogers (1971) and I too had read him with interest and enthusiasm, especially as I absorbed his ideas of respect and empathy for and with the 'client'. Both Freud and Rogers left an imprint on my mind that remains excitingly active to this day. So in 1978 my interest moved back across the years to those earlier readings and, from a very different position in life, I decided to start again — to re-birth myself. I now had a lot of experience to draw on: a marriage, the fathering of four children and years of teaching human relations studies to generations of students.

Living in the North West of England presented a problem: how to train, to get personal therapy, to study with like minded persons in a professional way; how to get professional supervision; how to gain the essential clinical experience to make me a sound and safe practitioner? The obstacles seemed insurmountable. There was little in the form of interest and training in psychoanalytical ideas in the North West of England at that time. In an earlier academic period, teaching youth workers, I had become interested in and responsible for teaching theories of group work, with special reference to the dynamics of human interaction at both a conscious and unconscious level. This involved experiential as well as theoretical activity. I had learned to be bold and unafraid of experiment in examining the feelings of people in group situations, including my own. I was to build upon this.

Two years training in psychodynamic psychiatry at the Uffculme Clinic in Birmingham got me started. It is worth acknowledging now the importance of this early beginning in psychotherapy training initiated at that clinic. It was a sign of the times. At last, an alternative to biological treatments for the mentally distressed was being advanced within the NHS. In the big provincial UK medical centres an old idea was being re-born. Birmingham was well ahead of most but a movement was in hand that would not be stopped. Synchronistic with all these developments was the emergence of a new class of psychiatrist: the 'Consultant Psychotherapist'. Psychodynamically trained, the brief of these specialists was to 'treat and to train', and relative to their numbers this 'new' profession has enjoyed much success in challenging the essentially conservative psychiatric procedures of their profession.

A significant side issue now emerged. With the establishment of the post of Consultant Psychotherapist as a medical psychiatric category, the insurance companies associated with the provision of private medical treatment, such as BUPA and PPP, began to fund psychotherapy in private practice. This was to have a spin-off effect later in the creation of counselling agencies, which provided support to employees of large bodies such as insurance companies and banks.

The Uffculme course was a product of new thinking and practice represented by these pioneering psychiatrists. After all, Freud (1926) had insisted that psychoanalysis was not a medical activity. I organized a heavy programme of both traditional and contemporary analytic reading and entered into a sustained experience of psychoanalytically based psychotherapy. The Uffculme training course offered a two-year experience of group analytic psychotherapy as an inclusive part of the training. Significantly, a lay therapist was employed to conduct our therapy group. How I envied him and hoped to emulate his achievements. As the Uffculme course concluded I complemented it with a further year of training in group analysis (Foulkes, 1957), which had just been inaugurated by a group of innovative psychiatrists in Manchester in association with the London-based Group Analytic Society.

It would be remiss not to acknowledge the growth of interest in the field of counselling that was emerging, at the same time as the renewal of awareness of the value of analytical psychotherapy and its potential in the treatment of emotional and mental disorders. Following the appearance in the UK of the innovative publications of Carl Rogers (1971), training courses in counselling were being established at all levels throughout the country. There was a great upsurge in interest and no lack of trainees. This was to indirectly benefit me when I got my first referral from a trusting university counsellor, trained at the Westminster Pastoral Foundation for Counselling. She provided my first 'client', who in turn gave me rich case material to take to supervision. During the therapeutic relationship with this first young woman I received strong support from the university counselling team and the university medical centre, with both of whom I established a good working relationship and this gave me a feeling of confidence; I was trusted.

She was shortly followed by a second client who had been dismissed from an NHS therapeutic community and was regarded as pretty well untreatable; she was described as having a 'personality disorder', being unresponsive to analytic psychotherapy (Feasey, 1998). These first two cases, which, I hasten to say, I took on without really realizing the difficulties I was to be faced with, provided truly sustaining and challenging experiences for me as a trainee psychotherapist. I am deeply indebted to both these clients for the therapeutic relationship I shared with them and the consequent learning that took place. I am also grateful to my supervisors who helped me to work therapeutically and safely with potentially dangerous material, to the benefit of both my clients and myself.

Around this time I was introduced to a woman group analyst/consultant psychiatrist who found a place for me as a therapist, albeit voluntary and sessional, in her day therapeutic community within an NHS hospital. This placement provided me with a depth and variety of clinical and supervisory experience that I could not have possibly obtained anywhere else, and which was quite invaluable! Another recommendation took me into further training and supervision with two very experienced American psychotherapists, one of whom was a consultant psychotherapist and psychodramatist, the other a lay psychotherapist, each of them specialized in group psychotherapy. So gradually I built up a programme of therapy and training and clinical experience, all of it coming together in a rather intense and demanding combination but at the age of 50 I had little time to lose. This book is not an autobiography so I must necessarily cut short any further consideration of personal professional development. I believe, however, that numbers of therapists and counsellors have trodden a similar path.

In approaching analytic psychotherapy or Rogerian counselling, the practitioner must realize that therapy is the product of a relationship, an alliance, and the principle instrument of therapy available to the therapist is the self. Indeed it is not only the principle instrument of therapy, it can also be the principle handicap to therapy. By the time I came to the conclusion that I could run a practice I had made some very important personal discoveries, not least that without being rigid or dogmatic I would work in the analytic mode of Freud and the humanistic liberality of Carl Rogers. Freud in the twentieth century was my inspiration. This was the 1970s, a time of liberality, free expression and experiment in lifestyles and therapies. Freud was a mentor but not a gaoler. Coming to that conclusion has had a profound effect upon my practice. From it I have discovered how a practice can be run. It has determined my relationship with my clients and helped me balance my life in psychotherapy with my family life as a husband, and as a father and grandfather. It has enabled me to conduct a social life in a way that is compatible with being a therapist in an urban community and has clarified the way that I should relate to friends and acquaintances, especially counsellors and therapists from other disciplines. These matters are all of concern to the aspiring counsellor and therapist. They are best acknowledged openly and clearly rather than experienced in confusion and ambiguity, and will be explored further in later chapters.

Eventually I qualified additionally as a dramatherapist and psychodramatist, where analytic thought inspired a lot of work I did in the creative therapies. I find I have much to thank Freud for, although I have reservations about being labelled a Freudian; his name can still be provocative, especially to some feminist friends and clients. I can, however, read Masson (1992) comfortably! Although attachment to a 'name' in analytic psychotherapy is not at all helpful, it is important to have a defined position and a point of view, a perspective from which to think intelligently about the needs of the client and the meaning of his/her presented problems or pathology. Otherwise we are likely to be more than usually influenced by deeply subjective prejudices and partialities, with which all of us are burdened and which are likely to act to the detriment of the therapeutic or counselling relationship.

I was fortunate to be coming to therapy training at about the same time as Carl Rogers was published in this country and the first early establishment of counsellor training programmes was taking place. So counsellors and the ideas of counselling have always had a place in my professional landscape along with dramatherapists, psychodramatists and art therapists. The boundaries between therapists were gradually liberalizing, encouraging exchanges of ideas and experience, diminishing rivalry and competition. Psychoanalysis is not in the possession of psychoanalysts. Rogerian counselling is not in the possession of the counsellors. Ideas, once published, enter the common culture and escape the clutches of the originator and author.

In this time there have been very important professional developments with the establishment of a number of training institutes across the whole range of psychotherapeutic approaches. From the establishment of these training organizations came a drive towards harmonization and regulation of training standards and professional and ethical codes of practice. Thus the United Kingdom Council for Psychotherapy came into being, which set out to meet these emerging aims. A parallel development was proceeding in the world of counselling. The training base was, and remains, different. The training of counsellors has come largely into the area of tertiary education. But there was a need for a validating body. Thus a new body came into being: the British Association for Counselling, which now registers professional counsellors as competent and ascribing to a professional code of practice. The British Association for Counselling also carries out important work in 'recognizing' training courses, and from this has naturally emerged various levels of training and training competences.

New entrants to the field of counselling and psychotherapy are entering an exciting and rapidly developing area of work. Whilst it is still very difficult to get a job there are nevertheless opportunities unique to our time. I never thought I should see the day when counsellors would be encountered in doctors' surgeries, and their services available through the NHS. Even more surprising is the presence of counsellors in clinical psychology departments. Increasingly, departments of psychotherapy, most of them working with a psychoanalytic orientation, are being set up by NHS Trusts around the country and training institutes for psychotherapy now exist in many parts of the country.

Apart from public provision there has come into being a growing area of private practice. New private hospitals have been established to provide a mental health service and they survive largely as a result of the provision of private health insurance schemes. Alongside these hospitals have come a small but increasing band of private practitioners in counselling and psychotherapy who, although having been trained in a variety of theories and techniques, have much in common. In this latter group are some who work entirely as stand-alone therapists and counsellors, whereas others combine some private practice with work in the health and social services. A colleague with a modest private practice, having just landed an NHS contract, said, 'Oh, thank goodness, now I'll get paid holidays, sickness benefit and a pension'. I know how he felt!

In the following chapters I set out what I conceive as guiding principles of practice for those setting out on the adventure of a professional career in counselling and psychotherapy, drawing together the common elements of both therapeutic approaches rather than emphasizing their differences. Certain topics will, of necessity, be dealt with only in passing, and readers may fruitfully follow up special interests in publications that deal in depth with their concerns. The bibliography should help. Membership of a professional body, indicating and confirming your competence to practise as either psychotherapist or counsellor, opens up the world of public and private practice and this book sets out to offer some help for the therapist/counsellor to work in either direction.

Chapter 2
Place

A room is the place where you hide from the wolves outside.
(Jean Rhys in *Good Morning, Goodnight*. Penguin, 1972)

I recall many years ago a young male client coming to my house for an initial interview. I opened the door to him and he stood, framed in the doorway, wearing a pair of deeply tinted sunglasses. I could not see his eyes, so there was no eye contact between us. I ushered him into the consulting room. We settled ourselves and after a few minutes I spoke to him of the difficulty of communication that existed between us. I could not see his eyes, but he could see mine. Was there a question of trust? After a brief pause he took off his glasses and launched into a bitter attack on a clinical psychology department in the South of England where he had gone for treatment, where he felt no trust was offered and where he could not respond in a trusting manner. 'That is why I'm going private', he exclaimed. He looked round appreciatively at my well-furnished sitting room where I work with clients.

It was as if he was looking for value for money, for being valued and seeing some evidence of it! He contrasted it with sitting in drab corridors or bleak waiting rooms when appointments were often delayed or postponed, without notice. He was very angry. In contrast he seemed to feel that my therapy room represented some assurance of serious concern. And that *is* what I am aiming toward. His personal financial circumstance was that of poverty, although he probably would not have used that term about himself. To pay for his treatment, as he saw it, he intended to become a vegan and he did. For a while his consequent loss of weight concerned, even alarmed me, but it levelled off and he was for the most part, physically very well. He lived on the very edge of society, taking only the most marginal of social welfare benefits. His relationship with officialdom was hostile, formal and elusive. He was extremely neurotic, in the 'old-fashioned Freudian' (Freud and Breuer, 1895) sense of that word. He had many phobias and he was quite homophobic, which made social relationships very difficult for him, indeed nigh on impossible. He abused alcohol. Although he was a father he could not live with the mother of the child; on the other hand he had a rather mechanical and arid sexual life with her which she tolerated rather than enjoyed. He would probably have been described as suffering from a personality disorder by a psychiatrist and, as a result, as being untreatable. After some weeks of fencing with me, a reluctant swordsman — or perhaps 'wordsman', he settled down to work and found sufficient money to pay me a modest fee.

I believe the room where we worked was, and became more and more, important to him. The therapy room is of prime importance (Coltart, 1993). It is a space in which the client will think the therapist has 'room' for him/her and his/her concerns exclusively. It is the secret, confidential world in which the therapist and client come together in a relationship which is unique and important. The room provides security. It must provide an atmosphere where risks can be taken, where the normal codes of social communication need not be strictly observed. It is a privileged area. It certainly was for my very disturbed client and his need for such a secure setting and milieu was palpable. As far as practical the room needs to be inviolable and a therapist or counsellor working at home, especially with a family to be considered, needs to think carefully about the impact on the household of a room virtually being 'out of bounds'. To have such a room, in what to all intents and purposes is also a family house, is highly unusual and requires a deal of adjustment for family or household members. As far as furnishing is concerned there are a number of schools of thought. There is the minimalist position. This requires only the barest furnishing, whereby the therapist remains relatively anonymous. The theoretical position is that the client should not be distracted by the possessions of the therapist; the therapist should remain as anony-mous/'unreal' as possible, only being available as a figure of fantasy. The other school of thought does not bother much with the issue of therapist revelation through the furniture and decorations in the room. Indeed if a visit is made to the Freud Museum in Hampstead, London, then it is apparent that Sigmund himself was not much concerned with the issue. My own view is that it is a matter of theoretical position and personal taste. Certainly any analytical therapist would deal with any 'transference' issues that arise, so comments concerning the therapist's possessions would be treated as material for therapy and discussed and analysed. In my view such occurrences usually prove productive and helpful. Indeed for my disturbed client the room and its pleasant, rather than affluent, furnishing was a source of pleasure in contrast with the clinical psychology depart-ments he had attended. I, and my room, enjoyed the positive transference. I would expect the counsellor to be less concerned with fantasy but careful to provide a pleasant, secure, relaxed meeting place for counselling to occur in. For my angry client the room was a source of reassurance as well as rich fantasy concerning my status in the world!

Sometimes the outcome of immediate untested assumptions can be serious. We all jump to conclusions on the slenderest evidence. I found it quite amusing that this client, a man of very slender means, judged me to be 'rich', while at the same time another male client, a businessman, confessed to me that he nearly failed to ring my doorbell because my car — an old stylish Renault 16 — struck him as being little better than a 'banger' and that determined my standing in his eyes. I was more than a little stung by his judgement: not because of the implications concerning my status but rather at his crass failure to recognize the interest and value inherent in my 'interesting' French car. I felt outraged by his insensitivity — I wanted to be seen as interesting! This led to some interesting discussion with my supervisor.

Of course the client coming into the therapist's or counsellor's house is, of necessity, coming into the therapist's life in an intimate way. Although a counsellor might not give so much space to the notion of transference, the presence of a client in the counsellor's 'private' space has to be acknowledged. All manner of consequences flow from that situation, some of which are relatively passive, coming into therapy through the fantasies that are brought to light in the therapeutic dialogue. A psychoanalytically oriented therapist will obviously work through the transference material that surfaces. A counsellor will probably find him- or herself reflecting on the sense of well-being or the sense of deprivation that the circumstances excite in the client. Some feelings that arise provoke action, whereby the client may try to discover more than the room immediately reveals by trying to see more of the premises, or by trying to meet the therapist's family.

An early client of mine, a young woman from a dysfunctional family, hung about outside the house in order to see my wife leaving the building. She then tried to talk to her. My wife behaved with courtesy and politeness. My client would always comment if my telephone rang during a session, imagining my wife would answer it; she confessed that sometimes she would ring when she thought I would be with a client in order to speak to my wife, her mother in fantasy. A sudden request to go to the lavatory for example often opens up the house or flat to further enquiry! It is pretty well impossible to refuse such a request. There is in all of us an urge to see and be seen. I recall that many years ago doctors would have stained glass panels in the waiting room windows to preserve anonymity. Some counsellors reading this may feel I am over-concerned with the reaction of clients to the consulting/therapy room and indeed may not acknowledge a need to deal with transference issues. I am convinced, however, that where a private household is utilized as the setting for therapy or counselling it is sensible to be wise to the issues for the sake of the client and counsellor/therapist alike. The past gulf between psychoanalytic therapists and counsellors concerning issues of transference and interpretation is, I am glad to say, closing. The therapists are allowing more reality into their relationship with the clients and the counsellors are acknowledging, more readily, the presence of fantasy and projection in their work with clients.

Clearly these arrangements are for the benefit of the client but the family, if there is one, may well look upon the scene with rather more anxious eyes. What exactly is going on in that room? Why should the family not see and meet the clients? Why should the clients have such priority in the therapist's life, sometimes to the detriment of the family? And so on. Envy and resentment towards the clients may be paramount and this is part of the price for the convenience of working at home and being a psychotherapist. If the therapist/counsellor feels that all these issues are too much to cope with then it might well be much better to find a room to rent in a therapy centre from which to work. The family will more easily accept the notion of the therapist going 'out' to work and see it as quite normal, and the feelings I have described are unlikely to arise in such intensity.

Given that the decision is to work at home in a private room, does it matter where the therapist sits? I was given some sensible advice by an experienced psychiatrist some years ago. 'Don', she said, 'don't let the patient sit between you and the door; that way you can always make a quick get away, should the need arise!' I was slightly surprised by this suggestion. It had never occurred to me that I might be at risk in the therapy room. The need to get out quickly has never arisen at home, but it might have done. I once had a client, a young woman, who would roam the room, ignoring my interpretations. She would sit on the floor beside my chair leaning heavily against it, just, but only just, avoiding physical contact with me. Her close presence could be oppressive. I do *not* sit behind the client as Freud did. On the contrary, I like to see body language. I do have a settee in my room and some clients like to occupy it. Some sit in a chair and some start with the chair and change to the settee after a few months of therapy. This is a matter of choice. The aim is for security and to provide a setting that 'holds' the client in a relaxed, free and introspective mood where any art objects, photos, paintings or whatever in the room are available for discussion; in other words, nothing is to be censored. Everything in the room is a subject for free association.

The home as a therapy place usually means that there is no waiting area. This affects the timing of appointments and the issue of confidentiality. Most private clients, in my experience, do not wish to be seen by other clients as they come and go for appointments. The appropriate way to deal with this situation is to arrange *at least* fifteen-minute gaps between appointments and to stress to clients that to preserve anonymity they should keep pretty strictly to the schedule. Obviously from time to time the arrangement falters but by and large it works. On the other hand, I have found that visitors staying in my home while I am still working will invariably choose to leave the house just at the moment a client is arriving, despite my courteous warnings and requests to leave *after* the client has arrived. Patience is required. But there appears to be a powerful voyeuristic element at play in most people which staying in the home of a psychotherapist can stimulate. I have tried not having visitors when practising, but this is simply impractical. Neighbours too need to be taken into account. No matter how discreet I may be I do not kid myself that the neighbours are not aware of my profession. On the contrary, they are very aware of what I do and notice the coming and going of my clients throughout the day. I am not sure that it matters very much except where the client is known to the neighbour, although from time to time I am able to be helpful to neighbours who are looking for a therapist — obviously not me! I would argue that even where a room in a therapy/counselling centre is being used it is not at all uncommon for other users to want to have a quick look at a client who is waiting for the appointment. It seems there is, in virtually all of us, a powerful voyeuristic element that cannot easily be denied. Charles Brenner, correctly in my view, locates this impulse within early sexuality (Brenner, 1957). A remnant of this impulse stays with us in adulthood and asserts itself whenever an opportunity occurs to see that which is normally forbidden. So my request to avoid the approaching client is defiantly ignored!

On a more mundane level I try to ensure that I give the clients some car-parking space so they do not invade my neighbours' territory, which can be a cause of friction. At one time I lived in a small narrow cul-de-sac which meant that I had to ban parking by my clients outside my house. This may seem a trivial point but it led to feelings of rejection, persecution and anger, both open and repressed when clients first experienced my obduracy in this respect. The golden rule is, of course, to acknowledge these feelings willingly and allow the client full freedom to explore the anger and disappointment. But the refusal of the therapist to budge can prove extremely frustrating to a client. I would go a little further in attempting to meet the reasonable demands of the client for somewhere to leave the car. Merely to 'interpret' is sometimes highly inappropriate and frustrating. As Freud allegedly said, 'sometimes a cigar *is* a cigar'. We all know that a car can be more than a car. Finally the use of a room at home has certain legal implications. For example, the Inland Revenue will make an allowance for the use of the room and for its furnishing and maintenance. Your house contents insurers should be told what you are doing professionally in case an accident occurs or some damage takes place in which a client is implicated.

I have always found these bodies understanding and helpful. Working at home has many advantages and I would not happily give these up without a great deal of persuasion, but nevertheless care must be taken and thought given to the implications that arise.

The location where you work is worth considering. I have always worked at home and tried to live near convenient public transport, both bus and railway. This has been for my own convenience but very often it has been useful to my clients. It will also determine to some extent the kind of clients you get. I live in a large university city and I get referrals to see students who rely on public transport and bicycles. I have also been fortunate to own a house in pleasant surroundings where there is a degree of privacy and urban noises are not intrusive. I would hate to work near an airport with a noisy flight path. Fortunately I have never had to share premises or use a centre where I would have little control over the conduct of the premises. My house is essentially a domestic place and is reasonably anonymous in its aspect; I do *not* put up a brass plate or advertise in any way, so a casual passer-by would have no idea of what the house is used for. The reader may think all these considerations are mundane but practical arrangements resonate very actively in the psyche of both therapist and client and I make no apology for mentioning them here.

A private house in a quiet road is pleasant and stimulates fantasy. A number of my clients have used fantasy about my house in a very rich and rewarding way. One man saw the house as like Kafka's Castle, full of mystery and unanswered speculations. He would rail against my refusal to 'let him in' to my life or to be absolutely specific concerning what was required from him in therapy. Sometimes he saw me as a prosecuting lawyer, sometimes as his defence attorney, sometimes as his judge, sometimes as a fellow prisoner, sometimes as his executioner. Another woman client saw the house as a place of sanctuary in an otherwise very threatening world.

More recently a client, herself a therapist, spoke of my house admiringly but when she went further into the feelings found envy. Sometimes even just getting to the house would be used by a client in a pathological way. Two examples come to mind. In one instance I was dealing with a case of major agoraphobia. The client was a young foreign woman married to an Englishman. There were no children. She was quite impeded by the phobia. She could not leave her house unescorted. Quite unrealistically she wanted her husband with her all the time. When she first came to me she was escorted by him to my door. She wanted him to wait in my house for her. I said no. He promised to call for her at the right time and did so. I lived then in the small cul-de-sac so I suggested for the next appointment he left her at the end of the road and she could then walk to my door. At first there was an absolute refusal but after some weeks of psychotherapy she agreed to do this. I next suggested she came in a taxi alone to the top of my road: at first refusal, then agreement. After about a year she was coming to me independently on foot, all the way from her house without an escort. This unfortunate, highly educated and intelligent woman had been sexually abused by a cousin during her adolescence. This cousin was a psychoanalyst! Now she had a psychoanalytic therapist to work with whom she could trust, the therapy room was safe and much painful resolution was to be made.

Readers will notice that I am not nervous of making 'behavioural' suggestions from time to time. This client was also shopping and generally getting around without an escort although there were still strong feelings of dependency. After another two years she was working as a languages teacher and she became pregnant and finished therapy. Some months later she stopped me in the street, an accidental meeting, and proudly showed me 'her baby'. She also thought of it as 'our baby': the creative product of therapy, not the mischance of rape. In this instance I saw this woman for an extended period of work and some readers might well question such longevity, but the essence of this contract was her desire to work in the long term and to free herself of debilitating dependency and anxiety. Time was needed. I believe many counsellors, who at one time would not have countenanced such a lengthy relationship, are now coming to see the need for long-term work This seems especially true when dealing with issues such as eating disorders and experience of sexual abuse in childhood. I would merely add that sometimes a continuing regime of therapy or counselling, practised regularly and conservatively, helps to provide structure in an otherwise chaotic life. I have found this to be particularly true when dealing with young clients who have to get out of bed to come and see me when they have turned day into night and night into day, which is not uncommon.

The other case was of a teenage girl who was 'sent' by her mother. She had to travel to my home town by rail and then walk to my house. At first she would ring me from *her* railway station and ask if I would fetch her. Then, this having failed, she would get to *my* railway station and ring me to come to get her. That failed too, so she would walk to within 300 yards of my house and telephone me from a public box with the same request. This also failed. She never got to me, although we had a number of telephone conversations. She failed and I felt I failed. I was younger and more rigid then than I am now. In my present circumstances I hope I would be creative enough to think of a compromise. Perhaps we could have split the journey from the telephone box to my house between us, each walking halfway, meeting in 'no-mans land'. At the time I was over-concerned with the rigid application of boundaries. I am sure Carl Rogers would have found a sensitive, sensible solution. The outcome for this young woman many years later was tragic and her death resonates with me to this day.

Much of what I have written does not apply so keenly if the counsellor/therapist is working in a therapy centre where he/she rents a room and enjoys the provision of a receptionist and message service. There may be definite advantages to such an arrangement but for myself I have always liked to be independent and to have the final say on the manner and place of my work. A number of my supervisees, both therapists and counsellors, have worked in rented accommodation and most of them have envied my consulting room: its comfort, privacy and the degree of control I have over the therapy situation. It reminds me of the contrast when working in a large NHS hospital where I never achieved a secure, inviolable room in which to work. After many shifts of location I ended up running a psychotherapy group in the ECT waiting room where technicians and nurses would breeze in and out without a murmur of apology or explanation! An NHS psychotherapist I am currently supervising took the post on condition that she was provided with a stable secure room to work in with patients and an understanding that her appointments were inviolable. She also insisted that the hospital trust paid for her to receive appropriate clinical supervision from outside the hospital staffing resources. And so I came on to the scene. The message is clear: if the therapist or counsellor receives an offer of employment from a hospital, day centre, GP practice or clinic, which in itself is not a specialist centre for therapy and counselling, then it is wise to set out the ground rules. It rests upon the informed therapist/ counsellor to do this rather than expecting this level of provision from an employer who may be quite ignorant of the requirements of therapy and counselling.

Lastly let me mention the telephone and the post. An answering machine is a *must* and it must be reliable. It is a bad thing when you think you have left a message on a machine if it fails in some respect and there is no record of such a message, a treacherous situation, so do not buy a cheap one. It must *not* be in the therapy room. Anyone living in the house must be ready to answer the telephone tactfully and cope with making appointments. The telephone is like an umbilical cord: it connects the therapist with the clients. A most dramatic example is as follows. A young woman, a student in residence at the local university, had cut herself up with a razor blade and painted her room with blood. She was rescued by a university nurse and taken hastily to the accident and emergency centre at the local hospital. In the casualty department she refused treatment until she had telephoned me, her therapist! She explained to a bewildered young doctor: 'You see I've broken my contract, I've damaged myself, I must be the first one to tell him'. She 'borrowed' ten pence from him to ring me as blood dripped onto the casualty department floor. This incident occurred in the very early days of my practice and I found it instructive, even amusing, in a dark comic way.

A less dramatic example is that of a severely disabled woman, a wheelchair user, arriving in her car. From just outside my door she used her mobile telephone to ring me for assistance in climbing two steps to get into my house. After some months she found the strength to give up the practice and found her own way in using crutches. At a later stage of this book I shall have a more to say about the use of the telephone and its 'place' in your work as a counsellor or therapist.

Finally, the post comes every day in some quantity. Delivered to the house, it arouses curiosity. But all post addressed to me is regarded as confidential. However, it can be provocative when a letter from a woman client comes *every* day, as indeed, in one instance, it did for a period of about six months. Arriving at a hospital or clinic these letters would have elicited only a clinical response and a certain curiosity from the secretarial staff. But arriving in my home their presence became intrusive and disturbing to family relationships. I could, as an analytic therapist, interpret the letters to my client but dealing with the matter inside the family was another matter. On one occasion only, I received an abusive anonymous letter. I found this letter most disturbing, especially as I was able to identify the typewriter upon which it had been typed, in my then place of work. If the therapist or counsellor is working in his/her own home then these missives from clients, whether of love or hate, resound on the doormat with an emotional thud. So, as Tom Lehrer sang in his satirical song, 'Be prepared! Don't be worried, Don't be flustered, don't be scared... be prepared!'. Take your concern to your supervisor.

When I first started this book I was not on the Internet email service. Now I am. I am intrigued by the possibility of clients trying to communicate with me via email letters, using the informal and easy manner of writing that the electronic medium seems to encourage. It is entirely a phenomenon of our time. The nearest to it for years was the now abandoned telegram; email is virtually instant and it comes to the therapist and sits on the computer screen waiting for a response: a reply by email! My view, at present, is that the reply, if it comes at all, will be in the therapy room as part of a therapeutic dialogue. I shall defend the therapy room and its special place in the relationship of client and therapist/counsellor and resist the appeal of the email letter, no matter how seductive it may appear to be. More will be said about this in the chapter on communications and confidentiality.

Chapter 3
Time

Time present and time past / Are both perhaps present in time future / And
time future contained in time past.
(T.S. Eliot in *Four Quartets*. Faber, 1962)

A young, very bright and intelligent client once looked at me with a
mixture of tease and irritation and said, 'All you bloody therapists are the
same: you're all obsessed with time, completely anal'. There is more than
a sliver of truth in this remark. I have known only a handful of analytic
therapists who are not strict observers of time in their practice. I certainly
am and it is central to my own practice. When I first came as a novice
patient to a psychotherapy group one of the things that impressed me
most was the tight discipline of time that was observed and exercised by
the group analyst. Time to close was observed, no matter what point we
had reached; as the moment came to finish, the session was closed by the
therapist, apparently with no hesitation or qualms. I soon discovered that
the structure of the hour, its beginning and end, constituted a framework
of work and safety for the members of the group. Then there is the famous
fifty-minute hour that is attributed to Freud, who gave himself a ten-
minute breather between clients, which is now revered as a part of an
analytic ritual, heavy with meaning and significance. The traditional way of
looking at the issue of the time in the therapy room is that late arrival
indicates a state of resistance, as does premature closing, which is more
rare. Remarks that are suddenly introduced in the closing seconds of the
hour are often seen as indicators of painful concerns, mentioned but given
no time to explore. Sometimes remarks are flung at us on the doorstep.
The therapeutic hour appears to hold together all our deeply subjective
feelings about time. These feelings are much in the province of analytic
psychotherapy and counsellors may have very varying attitudes and
practice in respect of time and its application to therapy. A group of
counsellors, whom I meet regularly for the purposes of supervision,
openly expressed pleasure when I took on the contract with them as their

supervisor, because as an analytic psychotherapist they knew I would keep to time. The majority of those I supervise treat time spent with clients with the respect it requires but often find it difficult to give time to their own benefit.

Does time exist? Is it an idea of those who invented clocks? Does time have a speed? How do we account for time flying and time dragging for us or for the client? Sometimes a minute seems like an hour, sometimes the hour like a minute. These experiences are just as much in the realm of the work of the counsellor as of the psychoanalytic psychotherapist, and deserve our attention. The counsellor or therapist in the first meeting with a potential client needs to address the issue of how the client makes use of time. Over-activity can merely indicate nervousness. Long silences often test the therapist's capacity to cope with pressure, and are sometimes of a manipulative character. Is the time 'well spent' — or is time 'wasted'? These questions need to be answered. A number of cameos illustrate this discussion.

The client I referred to in the opening paragraph, I shall call her Mary, would often subject me to the painful experience of an hour spent virtu-ally in silence. At first I imagined that time would hang like a dead cloud of nothingness; I dreaded the experience. But it was not at all like that. Time with Mary had much variation whether she spoke or not. I cannot explain that very easily. All I know is that in that hour of silence I would make one or two tentative interpretations which she would entirely ignore, but there would be an accompanying quality of time, charged or relaxed, fast or slow which cannot easily be understood. Perhaps I was unconsciously reading her body language and she mine. Certainly for her it was a novelty not to be attacked for being 'withholding' and 'manipulative'. I think she was puzzled by my response, that I did not attack her. I held on to the therapeutic position in the silence; I knew it was of vital importance. I was just as attentive to my own consciousness to prevent me from losing that 'free floating attention' so essential to the therapeutic relationship. Try as I may sometimes I would realize I could not account for the time that had passed: I had not slept, I had rather lost concentration and drifted into a coma-like state. This, an extreme example of the manner in which time — and how it was used — was so powerfully dramatized by silence. And this in a 'talking therapy'!

In great contrast I think of the client, previously referred to, who was over-active in the sessions. She would roam the room, sit on the floor, lean against the door, stand aloof yet threatening, looming over me. She would talk continuously, hardly pausing for breath, ignoring any interventions I might make. Sometimes a genuine exchange would start between us as the therapeutic hour was coming to a close; most frustrating. However, I knew she was entirely respectful of the time boundaries of the session and would leave, as she came, on time. This was a relief, not only to me but also to her. These two cases are illustrative of the extremes of experience; most are not so polarized. Nevertheless, the context of therapy is bounded by time and notions of time wasted or time usefully employed are central to the relationship of counsellor, therapist and client. I hope both of these examples illustrate the importance of time as boundary, in its emphasis both on starting and closing a session.

Time in therapy and counselling has another meaning, which is related to frequency and length. First of all the issue of frequency is a contentious one. My practice is often to settle at an agreed *minimum* of once a week for an hour at a time, although this may vary as therapy comes to a conclusion. The conclusion of the therapy is sometimes extended into a period of fortnightly sessions. My maximum has been four times a week (I work four days a week), which is what it became with Mary. Paradoxically, in response to her silence in the early days of therapy where we met once a week, I asked her to increase her attendance. My view then was that if she did not come virtually every day then she would probably end up in the local mental hospital. She came very faithfully. Frequency is a matter for negotiation. There is sometimes an anxiety that analytic psychotherapy will destabilize a particularly fragile or vulnerable client. This must be a matter of professional judgement, but it is often the case that *more* not less therapy should be the order of the day. Money comes into this situation. A client may well be able to afford to come once a week paying something like £25 per session. But to come twice or three times a week at a multiplying cost is impossible. A way of dealing with this is to negotiate a weekly fee. More will be said about this in a separate chapter.

For counsellors, working from a different training culture and within the restraints of institutional practice, to offer increased attendance or even a regular once a week meeting is questionable. Indeed, in this situation counsellors may well have been chosen by the client because he/she may want a relatively brief encounter. The issue of client choice is a real one and should be respected in the first instance. On the other hand, many counsellors faced with this situation do so only to discover that it is simply the overture to a more deeply engaged relationship where more time is required. Sometimes the counsellor can respond to the request safely and successfully, sometimes not. Painful compromises are then required, or another referral must be made, for the client's benefit. It rests on counsellors and therapists not to deny the significance of what sometimes is being practised in the name of management or finance, rather than good counselling and therapy.

I use the full hour for therapy. Frankly, when I read about Freud's punishing regime of work (Jones, 1964) I was appalled. I determined to see no more than five people in a day; it is usually less than this. At the rate of four to five clients in a day I felt quite able to give the clients a full hour and to take at least a quarter of an hour's break between appointments. This has proved satisfactory and I vary the time only for supervisees, whom I see for one and a half hours, or for the rare, but interesting, work that I sometimes do with couples, families or groups. Time is related to the size of the group and is negotiable, usually an hour and a half. The important principle is to provide security and predictability for the clients and personal leisure, or 'creative recovery' time for the therapist. In any case, although the better part of a therapist's time is spent in face-to-face work, time has to be found to read, to write, to consult and to continue training or supervision or personal therapy. For the independent therapist and counsellor working alone it is vitally important that issues of isolation be addressed and compensated for in some manner, such as finding time to be with agreeable others! The therapeutic context stretches beyond the intimacy of the consulting room. More will be said about this in a later chapter.

A more mundane matter is the question of clocks. Let there be one that is clearly seen by the client and therapist alike. I admit to being a clock-watcher; my own obsessive tendencies are reflected in this concern, but I think 'keeping an eye on the clock' is the therapist's duty and the client's more subjective concern. So, let the clock be obvious and clear so that there is no need for glancing furtively at a wristwatch. Clocks and time can be of great significance to my clients. A client recently launched a pretty heavy attack upon my time-keeping arrangement and the way that I closed sessions promptly. He saw this as evidence of a non-caring attitude and a desire on my part for control at the expense of concern. The two clocks in the room were out of sync by about two minutes! The clock he saw was two minutes behind the clock that I could observe and so the session closed with him losing two minutes of my/his time. All this was good thera-peutic material and together we recognized his protest as being signifi-cant, needing attention. The client's response to the use and control of time is often a very evident description of such experiences as childhood separation, with its consequent emotional deprivation and anxiety (Winnicott, 1958). There is often then a strong need felt to control the coming and going of the therapeutic meeting. The ability of the therapist to 'hold' the client within a sustainable therapeutic relationship, sometimes symbolized by time, is critical. Time is an essential component of the situation. Hence the popular expressions: 'He wouldn't give me the time of day' or 'I've no time for him' or, conversely, 'I've always got time for him and he for me'.

A client recently went to the library to read up about analytic therapy and what he could look for in my performance. Time was a feature he particularly focused upon. Associated with it were also concerns about me 'giving him the time of day' and 'having time' for him. He was pleased too that he could see my name in the book he was reading; as a result I met his expectations and he thought of me as a 'proper' therapist. Of course, for me all this has transference implications and my view is that all our performance in therapy carries this loading of significance. Counsellors may not pay much heed to the theoretical significance of transference but my experience of working with them for many years shows that they invest the relationship with the client with importance, understanding its significance in the counselling process from another perspective. The client who discovers in the therapeutic relationship someone who provides sufficient time experiences a gain that will resonate back through the past to the most critical experiences of psychic development. A counsellor going into private practice for the first time will soon discover that he/she is likely to become a very important figure in the life of his/her clients and this phenomenon needs addressing consciously, so that it may figure in the counselling therapeutic relationship.

How long should therapy last? How long is a piece of string? Therapists have been accused of hanging on to clients and creating a culture of dependency. There is some truth in this accusation, especially where the matter of money comes into the picture. A client leaving takes away income, a painful thought and experience for the therapist in private practice. Freud spoke of 'flight into health'; it is undoubtedly true that some — a few — clients finish therapy prematurely, but in my experience not very many. However, when it happens it can be quite wounding. A well-established professional man came to see me recently who had psychotherapy qualifications, and I suggested we met three times before making a contract. He came three times and seemed happy with the relationship between us. He made another appointment and left. I received a telephone call from his secretary a few days later cancelling the appointment and telling me that my client would ring to make another appointment with me. I have never seen or heard from him again. He has not responded to two brief courteous letters of enquiry. I have not been paid for the missed appointments. So he hurt me in a number of ways. I experienced the loss of confidence that must come from this kind of unexplained and unconsidered rejection, a narcissistic wound. I also lost out financially. There was also a residue of anxiety left in me concerning my client's welfare; I had thought him to be needy, requiring therapeutic attention.

It is a normal procedure for the client to suggest a finishing date and sometimes the therapist finds him/herself alluding to the end of therapy in a therapeutic context. The therapist/counsellor needs to monitor this feeling in him/herself, and perhaps take it to supervision. Sometimes there is an urge to be rid of a particularly difficult (for us) client. The issue needs attention. But one must not ignore the capacity to hate the client, or to love, for that matter. Counter-transference in the therapist is always active and we are capable of endless rationalization to avoid recognizing its influence. How long, then, should therapy last? I think it is rare for a client to come to my practice for less than a year. Mary came for an initial three years while she read for a degree, then she took a job some way away but after a break of about four years came back into therapy for some further two years. I do not regard this as exceptional, although Mary was a particularly damaged person who needed a long sustained period of psychotherapy to survive and grow, which she did. Her time in therapy was organized in two stages and for her that was quite appropriate. The break in between was a time of further growth and development and consolidation of the work she did in her first stage of therapy, so I was quite happy to see her return.

Recently a mature women client announced without much advance notice that she intended finishing therapy. I was rather surprised. She was difficult to work with in one particular respect. She is a woman of high intelligence and professional accomplishment. She has achieved success largely through skilful cognitive and behavioural management of her professional life, and she is much respected for her position by those around her, including her family. But as a client these very qualities sometimes impeded progress. For the most part she kept her feelings in check. When she decided to leave I decided to challenge her decision in a strong emotional way: I made it clear that I thought her decision was premature and there was much more to do in our relationship with each other; I interpreted her wish to leave as a 'flight into health' and said it was a way of escaping emotional exposure both to herself and to me. She left the session pretty angry with me, thwarted in her desire to leave with the permission that I would not give. Some days later she rang me, asking to come back to discuss the issue further. I welcomed the approach and she came back into therapy. I am glad to say that when she finished therapy with me, some six months later, she acknowledged with gratitude my intervention to prevent what would have been a premature conclusion.

I often say to clients who are leaving that they should resist a telephone call to me for a premature return. Time may need to pass before a fruitful return can be accomplished. In a general sense, people understand that human beings do make adjustments and accommodations with the passing of time and many a broken heart has mended as the weeks, months and years go by. Psychotherapists and counsellors need to understand this simple but profound human process, which may be incorporated into therapy in a positive way if it is recognized and used with sensitivity.

There are counsellors and some psychotherapists, especially those working in the NHS or for Social Services, who may be bound to a time framework not of their own making. Ethically the client should be made aware of the time span and frequency on offer so that he/she is not working in ignorance of the constraints. Often good work can be done which may act as a prelude to further therapy at another time, place and in a different circumstance. The issues of time between sessions of therapy and the continuing of therapy to its conclusion are worth consideration.

Is there no place for time-limited psychotherapy or counselling? Of course there is. A number of studies have indicated the possibility of benefit deriving from relatively short, time-limited therapeutic interventions (Guthrie et al., 1998). The issue is not of what is right and what is wrong but rather what is appropriate. A counsellor working within the framework of limited sessions, either by choice or necessity, needs to be aware of the client's expressed needs and the clinical needs of the condition that has brought him or her to the counsellor's attention in the first place. Where more time is needed and the counsellor or therapist cannot provide it, the professional requirement is to help the client find the necessary therapeutic relationship elsewhere. We all know, from our own experience, that brief interventions may be very significant in our life space. There can be no absolutes in this matter. There may be, too, a desire by either counsellor or psychotherapist to hang on to a client to postpone the day of separation. Whatever the rationalization, this is usually an indication of some personal pathology.

Where a therapeutic relationship is established, sensitivity to time is required in another way. Sensitivity here means knowing how to use time to the best advantage, especially in respect of interventions. An analytic therapist has to know the right time to challenge or to interpret or clarify or inform. Analytic psychotherapy is an active therapy; it is not only reflective. Sometimes clients experience this as a shock, particularly if they have picked up notions of non-interventionist counselling where reflective dialogue is more usually employed. More and more clients come to therapy informed, sometimes misleadingly so, concerning the world of therapy and counselling. Paradoxically, years ago, the client looked for direct intervention from the therapist towards sorting out the most subjective of emotional states. Psychoanalysts or psychotherapists were sometimes accused of not doing enough to help their clients through helpful suggestion. With the coming of Carl Rogers (1971) and his message of unconditional regard, empathy and reflective counselling, the accusation is now sometimes of over-activity by the analyst. A rather worn-out counsellor said to me recently that she was fed up with waiting for her client to address the issue of sex in her current non-sexual 'live-together partnership'. This was the third occasion in which a partnership had withered into a state of frustrating non-sexual existence but somehow it never came up as an issue. I suggested she address the woman's defences directly. The counsellor grinned at me wearily and riposted, 'Oh that's OK for you, you're an analyst; I couldn't possibly do that'. I continued, rather spitefully, 'Well, you will just have to wait, won't you?'. We both laughed. She then spoke ruefully of 'taking it to supervision'. But the timing of the process of making an active interpretive intervention that challenges a powerful defence system has to be right. The right time has to be found and in this book I cannot tell the reader when that time will arrive. Sometimes waiting for the right time means a long wait, sometimes the moment comes quickly. Therapists and counsellors are not gods, they make mistakes and getting the timing wrong is something we all experience. My own experience tells me that when the timing of an interpretation is wrong or inappropriate its sinks like a stone to the bottom of a pond. Counsellors may find themselves 'waiting for ever' in frustrated impotence, but that does not mean we cannot try to get the dialogue going again, or even again and again.

Timing is often a matter of patience, persistence and resilience. The client too often needs to find the right time to talk about a long-suppressed and censored subject and when that moment comes the therapist needs to synchronize his/her timing to make the best use of an opportunity. I recall the pain and inadequacy I felt when an elderly women finally described being raped by hostile soldiers as the war came to an end in Eastern Europe in 1945. She had been 'in therapy' with me for over a year and it had taken that long to find the trust and confidence to speak and reveal her lifelong secret. Again, I had been pursuing what Freud (1974) described as 'free-floating attention', that which is not dominated by the therapist's priorities but rather is available to resonate with the client's. But like a lot of Freud's injunctions this one is more easily understood than practised and I found myself regretting the time that had passed. Both counsellors and therapists need to recognize that, whatever our conscious intentions, we give off unconscious signals to our clients that encourage or discourage them from revelation.

What of the therapist's day? How available should he/she be to clients? I cannot prescribe this. Sufficient for me merely to say that my working day finishes at 6.15 p.m. My working week starts at 9.00 am on Tuesday and finishes on Friday afternoon at 6.15 p.m. This has led to me losing some clients who otherwise might have worked with me if I had been more flexible in my working time. But for me it was important to keep the priorities of my life focused where they had always been, on time given to family life, recreation and personal relationships. I have been reassured by the fact that I have for some 20 years had an interesting private practice which has produced a reasonable and satisfying financial reward as well as giving me time for other concerns. I could have worked longer or more flexible hours and earned more money. Other therapists and counsellors I have supervised offer evening appointments or work over the weekend, especially beginners striving to get a private practice off the ground. It must be a matter of personal choice depending on personal circumstances. On the other hand, it is inarguable that if the therapist is going to survive as a human being then time has to given to personal recreation and to experiencing the positive qualities of relationships with others. In the last five years I have seen two experienced therapists collapse into serious breakdown and another commit suicide. They were renowned for their hard work and devotion to the needs of clients. They gave little or no attention to their own life needs until the situation got out of control and in one case that was far too late. Ironically the latter therapist was a keen advocate of spiritual regeneration and self-preservation. Thus, whatever the particular situation of the therapist it has to be borne in mind that we work in a high-risk profession and we need to give close attention to signals of stress or disorder. Recently I discovered that a senior colleague, an experienced therapist and counsellor, had been taking medication to help with sleep disturbance for more than two years.

So time has to be found for our own therapy. It is not uncommon for psychoanalysts to refresh their personal therapy at regular intervals in their lives. Perhaps counsellors could learn from that tradition. The more recently trained therapists seem not yet to have learned the necessity for this scrutiny and self-appraisal. There is a tendency for psychotherapists trained and working in the NHS to take a position of distance from their patients, not to understand and accept that personal neurosis may occur in anyone in any position at any time and especially at moments of stress in personal relationships. To give time and attention to ourselves through the medium of a therapeutic relationship at significant moments of change in our lives seems merely sensible, not an admission of weakness or psychic incompetence. It is ironic that people working in the health professions seem to experience so much difficulty in dealing with their own health.

In addition, as therapist and counsellors, we are likely at any time to be the targets of unexpected neurotic attack from almost any quarter. At a party recently I came under an angry attack after I had made an offhand remark about sex. I was taken aback, and tried to defend myself very unsuccessfully. I was rescued by a woman friend, who said: 'Well, what do you expect — you are a man and a psychoanalytic psychotherapist, a perfect target'. I think most of us forget this truism and behave as if we are invulnerable and can cope with almost anything all of the time. In hospital and day clinics the medical model tends to encourage an 'us' and 'them' situation in which the therapist is and always will be well and the patient unwell. The therapist or counsellor working in the NHS needs time for support that is often not forthcoming from managers and employers. I think the growing number of counsellors working in GP surgeries are in danger of falling into the same spirit of denial, as indeed do many of the doctors they work for. Personal therapy time is expensive, too, often seen as pertinent only in the training setting and rarely resorted to until and unless a personal crisis occurs. Time spent in personal therapy is valuable time, time well spent. Supervision obviously plays a part in dealing with this problem and sometimes it borders very closely on therapy and in itself maybe sufficient. I hope I have made my point.

My awareness of time is not simply, as my client suggested, because I am anally obsessed with the control of all issues. It is rather that within the therapeutic situation it plays an important role and often spells out the position of the client at any moment of time vis-à-vis the therapist and the world about them. 'Time passing' gives us a context in which to appraise ourselves and 'time to come' helps us to engender hope for new tomorrows when we might encounter encouraging experiences. This applies to therapist and client. As I write I have just finished a session with one of the most silent and depressed of my present clients. He seems quite stuck in an unchanging world of apathy, sadness and depression. We struggle together with hope for the future and with a desire to understand and accept the meaning of the past. In a sense we could say that 'time is the essence of our contract'. I hope we shall stay together until sufficient time has been given to the therapy and he has reached a position where the 'stuckness' will be a thing of the past and he will be living in a dynamic healthy relationship with the possibilities of the future.

Chapter 4
Referrals and assessment

Don't let your opinions sway your judgement.
(Sam Goldwyn. Quoted in Pepper, 1985)

Starting as a psychotherapist or counsellor immediately raises the question, 'How do I get a client?'. If the therapist is in a training situation then, if he/she is lucky, a referral may be forthcoming from the institute he/she is training with but this is not always the case. Far from it, as very often the trainee, and most counsellors, must fall back on their own resources to find a suitable client. Or, paradoxically, an institute may provide a referral service for its trainees but not for its graduates, at least not in an organized, formal way. So the trained, qualified therapist/counsellor is suddenly alone in the world looking for a client or, it is hoped, clients. Of course if he/she lands a job in the NHS then the problem of finding a client disappears, only to be replaced by other, perhaps more serious challenges to good psychotherapeutic and counselling practice, where contact hours are governed by NHS budgets and facilities are at a premium. The client arrives, and then comes the business of assessment. But more of that later.

It is a real problem. An hour before starting to write this chapter I had a trainee therapist mulling over the significance of her only client. She was concerned not only with counter-transference issues but also with the iconographic importance of this client in relation to the demands of her training course. Without the client the course would lose much of its meaning to the young therapist and her personal learning would be seriously impaired. Within the client were embodied many of her hopes and aspirations towards meeting the training demands of her institute, and ultimately of becoming a good therapist. If she failed in the relationship with this client then it would be felt as a devastating blow to her self-esteem, both personal and professional. She was in danger of over-investment in this client and in that respect she was at risk. On the same afternoon I had a trainee male client who was bewailing the fact that he might have 'lost' a client through his own failure to keep an appointment. The issues here are many but I was struck by the way the client was described over and over again in terms of qualifying hours (time again!) required by the training course. It was almost as if the client was hated for his significance in the trainee's life. Training courses contain and often hold to themselves the primary clinical values for the trainee, and in this case it was 'qualifying hours', as defined by the institution, that ruled the day. For counsellors in training there is the endless struggle to achieve sufficient, supervised training hours of client contact to satisfy the demands of the British Association for Counselling. A supervising counsellor or therapist has two levels of concern. First, there is the responsibility to the trainee that his/her work is properly scrutinized and evaluated, and professional guidance provided to ensure good practice and learning; second, there has to be an equal regard for the client in respect of whom there should be no abuse of bad practice as a result of incompetence or neglect. In good practice it is client needs that occupy the high ground of concern and are the basis for ethical thinking on the part of the therapist, counsellor and supervisor. For the psychotherapist or counsellor in private practice the material value issue focuses upon money and the size of the practice; for the trainee it becomes hours of training value.

The issue of referrals is a complicated one and for the practising counsellor and psychotherapist in private practice it is a critical one. Apart from the psychological aspects there are the practical ones of economy: making a living, being able to finance personal and professional development, knowing how much to charge, dealing with personal moral issues which arise when a deserving client cannot pay. The issues are endless and do not go away with experience, although the therapist may become more skilful at dealing with them. In a later chapter I shall consider this issue at greater length.

And what of the psychotherapy/counselling trainee who comes as a client? The requirement of many training bodies now is that the trainee enters into therapy or counselling. At one level, for the accredited counsellor/therapist, this is a desirable development providing another area of gain, socially, materially and psychologically. But in my experience there is more to it than this. Most referring training bodies have requirements and want the trainee to experience the right kind of therapy and not come to grief with 'the wrong kind of leaves on the line'! The aim is to pass on the culture unchallenged by any heresy (Feasey, 1998). Again it is up to the individual to decide how much he/she wishes to bend to the requirements of the training organization. I know of one that actually insists that all the training therapists belong to that training body. Another I have worked with very happily has left it to the good sense of the trainee to make a suitable choice for him/herself, the only limitation being that the training therapist be fully accredited by the United Kingdom Council for Psychotherapy (UKCP) within the appropriate section. Whatever the arrangement, the principle of therapy must remain the same: the client and the client's need determines the nature of the therapeutic relationship. The needs of any 'organization' should be secondary. The counselling culture sometimes confuses this principle when, in the course of training, trainee counsellors are introduced into personal development groups which are run by staff who are also responsible for teaching, evaluation and finally 'passing' the trainee in the award of a diploma. The confusion of roles is inescapable. It is inevitable that the training values of the course will penetrate this arrangement. Trainees will, either consciously or unconsciously, monitor what they say and how they express themselves in relation to the perceived position and role of the group conductor. Hence censorship, based on anxiety and the fear of failure, will enter the group and subvert its purposes. It is obvious, in this instance, that it is probably the financial management of such courses that does not allow the employment of an 'outside' conductor to provide a properly secure and confidential experience for the trainee counsellors. This may be unavoidable but the conflict of interest inherent in the situation, as I have described it, should be recognized by all concerned.

My own practice is fed by referrals from former clients and from other professionals. It is, roughly, evenly balanced. But then I have been in practice for nearly twenty years. What if you are just starting? And how does it start?

Usually it begins with a telephone call and after a short introduction by the caller I find myself saying, 'And how did you come by my name?', and in this way I suppose I betray my own anxiety. My practice tends to suffer from a famine and flood cycle, and sometimes I think I shall never get another referral and I become somewhat paranoid in a minor way. Thoughts such as 'No one thinks I am any good any more' or 'The competition is getting too hot, I am going to get out of this, I'm not up to this' fly through my head. I challenge them rationally. Then the telephone rings too often and I feel overwhelmed. In the flood situation it is all too easy to turn away a 'difficult' client, to find reasons not to take someone on, rather than face the real reason: that you have reached your limit in terms of therapy time in any one week and enough is enough. It is rare to have a waiting list and there are good reasons for not having one. A waiting list means that you are not meeting the client's wishes at the point of time when they are expressed. A waiting list can mean that instead of referring the client on to another competent therapist you are saving up the client to fill a space when your practice shrinks and your self-confidence and income are threatened. More often than not it is possible to find a private therapist or counsellor with vacancies to call upon when your list is full.

It is wise to face the issue of grandiosity, reminding yourself you are not God's gift to the therapy or counselling profession and that there are equally good therapists available in the area in which you live. Another issue lurks here and that is the question of client choice. At this juncture I might suggest that it is the duty of a psychotherapist or counsellor to build up a network of therapists and counsellors in different parts of the country to whom referrals may be made. Sometimes clients, through force of circumstances, have to change address and location and if you, as the therapist in the first instance, can make a safe and confident referral than that is all to the advantage of your client. Often clients are left to their own devices in finding a new therapist or counsellor. Some clients are quite open about the manner in which they are looking for therapeutic help and will tell you that they are going around seeing various therapists and counsellors to get a feel of what is available. This is disconcerting, but seems to me a way of finding therapy that starts from the client empowering him/herself.

Sometimes a client has to submit to the inexorable referral system of the NHS where it would be regarded as unacceptable for a client to sample the therapists on offer. How refreshing it would be if a client were enabled by being given the requisite information and guidance through which a choice may be made. Even something as simple as choosing the gender of the therapist or counsellor would be modestly empowering for the client. Sometimes a client would prefer to see a psychotherapist or counsellor with formal medical or clinical psychology training. I suspect that, in reality, a service based on analytic principles that was faced with a patient demand for choice might pull the old trick of outflanking the patient by making an interpretation of the patient's defences and consequent resistance. Counselling practices are probably free from this particular manipulation of the client/therapist relationship. On the other hand, when 'famine' reigns it is easy to convince oneself that the most 'unsuitable' client will benefit from psychotherapy or counselling. The notion of 'unsuitable' client is in itself a very contentious one and is not easily resolved (Feasey, 1998), so the danger is that the needs of a faltering psychotherapy practice will press hard when and where doubt exists.

In the case of the telephone call I am assuming that the client is making a direct approach. He/she has probably heard my name mentioned somewhere, often from a one-time client, or may have got my name from the UKCP or the British Association for Counselling (BAC) register. A few contact me from the *Yellow Pages* telephone directory, the only place where I am allowed professionally to advertise my services. My experience of enquiries from this source is that they are rarely productive of clients willing and able to work consistently in therapy. I will say more about this when discussing the issue of advertising.

Problems arise when relatives take the initiative. This sometimes occurs when the potential client is a teenage son or daughter. This is not an uncommon occurrence, and a therapist's reaction can vary a good deal. My own is quite straightforward. I insist that the approach should be made to me directly by the young person him/herself after a parent — mother or father — has rung me with the first anxious enquiry. This may seem a hard approach and undoubtedly a referral may fail at this stage but my view is that if the young woman or man makes the initial appointment directly, in a telephone call to me, the chance of establishing a therapeutic relationship is greatly enhanced and ultimately this will be of benefit to the client. In the first instance it is essentially symbolic. I am saying to all the parties involved that I work directly for my client, that that relationship is inviolable and that I am not going to be manipulated by third parties, no matter how well intentioned the communication might be. The growing number of counsellors in universities know quite well that direct approaches from their, often teenage, clients is the norm. Of course worried staff will, from time to time, approach the counselling department and when they do it is usual for the counsellors concerned to stress the need for the young person involved to make a direct approach on his/her own behalf. Recently a counsellor was telling me of a senior academic who, fearful of the consequences, asked the counsellors to inform a student that he was failing the course and would have to withdraw from the university! This counsellor was reminded in this instance that the university pays her salary; she is an employee. From an ethical and 'good practice' point of view, circumstances may easily arise that could bring her into conflict with her employing institution. In this case she did not hesitate to remind the professor that dealing with the formalities of academic failure was his responsibility.

The question of advertising arises. How can people get to know about you and what you have to offer? My parent institute bans advertising other than a simple insert in the *Yellow Pages* to which I have already referred. I expect readers realize that doctors in private practice are allowed to advertise in this way. Other than through professional registers I have no other means of attracting clients from the population at large. This restriction certainly does not apply to some other psychotherapists and counsellors and a number of competent counsellors I know regularly advertise in *The Big Issue*. My attitude to the *Yellow Pages* is mixed. When my practice was first set up I appeared in the appropriate section. Mine was a solitary item. There were no other therapists in my district. The result of this advertisement was a fairly regular flow of enquiries followed by assessments that came to nothing, which was disheartening for the potential client and discouraging to me, although it put money into my practice. A tiny minority of enquirers became ongoing clients and worked to a good ending. I withdrew from the *Yellow Pages* the following year, but even now I have some regrets. It is obvious that some rather naive and needy clients are cut off from possible therapeutic gain by their inability to 'find' me. Often their GPs are not sympathetic to analytic psychotherapy and regard the private sector as populated by 'quacks' and exploiters. In these circumstances some clients are driven to the *Yellow Pages* as their only source of information. I can only leave it to the individual discretion of readers to settle this matter for themselves, bearing in mind any guidelines that they may need to observe laid down by their training agencies or psychotherapy institutes. I am once more actively considering a 'free' advertisement in the *Yellow Pages* in the belief that the public now appears to be a little more sophisticated in its appreciation of the possibilities and limitations of therapy and counselling. I do have another way of advertising myself, which is by keeping up a steady flow of articles in a number of therapy journals. This keeps my name in view of other professionals who may refer to me. Other people I know go to conferences and courses to 'keep in the swim' professionally and to be 'known'. But this is not for me. However, it seems a quite legitimate manoeuvre in the business of being known.

Over the last few years a new and progressive development has taken place in relation to the support of employees who may need psychological help. Employee Assistance Programmes are now quite common, especially in the field of big business, i.e. banks, insurance companies, airlines and so on. In response to this concern there are now professional counselling companies who act as a go-between, putting the employee in contact with the counsellor. I am not a counsellor and I do not offer relatively short-term work, but on occasions the referring agency looks for a psychotherapist who is prepared and equipped to work in depth with a client for a substantial period of time. More often than not this can be provided by a psychotherapist who is 'on the books' of such a referring body. Mostly there are no real difficulties because the referrers are themselves skilled and experienced in the field of psychotherapy and counselling and know how to distinguish between the two without getting sucked into issues of rivalry and competition. I must admit that in the past I have treated such overtures with some suspicion, fearful that the employer may try to call the tune and put pressure on me directly or indirectly, through the client, to work towards outcomes that would not necessarily be of my or the client's choosing. I am glad, however, to say that this has not been my experience and one employer met my fees himself through an insurance agency for over two years. All I was required to do was to provide an annual clinical report agreed upon between me and the client. At the end of the two years my client paid the therapy fees himself. Another client I worked with for some three years, to a reasonably successful outcome, came to me after experiencing a massive psychotic episode of a classical paranoid character derived from confusion concerning his sexual identity. His employer never ceased to support him and I felt fully trusted and empowered in my way of working with him, whilst at the same time he received lithium therapy through the auspices of a supportive psychiatrist. But the outcome is not always successful and the only client I have ever worked with who killed himself came to me through an employee-assistance department. In this instance the client himself was very reluctant to accept the nature of his engulfing depression and regarded the employer's attempts to help with suspicion, and insisted on holding me at bay despite all my efforts to create a trusting and therapeutic relationship. For some time after this experience I found myself wondering whether my collaboration with the employer had been based on a sound relationship of concern for the client. Freud is reputed to have said that 'every symptom has an aim' and in this instance I felt the death of this client very keenly. I could only compensate by offering support to his partner, which I did when she contacted me as she tried to come to terms with his devastating attack upon the relationship. Such are the complications that face a therapist in situations of deep and confusing ambiguity. It needs to be borne in mind that therapists do not operate in some kind of capsule of concern, rather they are inevitably linked to the 'outside' world by a network of emotional and social concerns that weave a pattern of care and anxiety around the therapeutic relationship. The parameters are sometimes very uncertain.

I would like to stress here how a sound working partnership has developed between me and a number of individual counsellors who in turn work with counselling agencies, and an increasing number of my referrals come from them via their agency to my practice. Counsellors coming new into the field of private practice need to realize that the agencies require them to be fully accredited by the BAC and that in general the work is of a short-term nature. Where further therapeutic work is required the client is referred on, at his/her own expense, to an independent practitioner, counsellor or psychotherapist, whichever is most appropriate.

An independent 'working alone at home' therapist/counsellor has to accept the fact that when the telephone rings and a potential client books an exploratory appointment he/she is inviting a stranger into his/her home. Behind my question 'And who gave you my name?' lies this concern. After all, the person calling may be a stranger straight off the street and there is a need to react with proper, sensible caution. I am usually reassured when the enquirer mentions an ex-client. I know this person who is coming will already have had some account of me. I also know my former client will have decided that the enquirer and I may well suit each other. This kind of referral is so different from that which comes via a doctor, psychiatrist or referral agency where there will already have been some assessment made of the suitability of the client for therapy and the suitability of therapy for the client! I am not suggesting one is better than the other, rather they are quite different. Each comes trailing clouds not of glory but rather expectation.

It could be argued, and probably is, that when an ex-client refers a friend to a counsellor or therapist, what is being enacted is an unfinished transference relationship: that the former client is still 'in love' with the counsellor or therapist and is likely to idealize the former relationship. This may be true but it does not in itself invalidate the action of referral. On the other hand, it may lead to disillusion! At the point of first meeting the therapist or counsellor is presented with the task of making an assessment. Where the client is coming with a warm endorsement of the therapist's skill from a former client there is obviously a danger that the therapist in question may find his/her assessment coloured in favour of working with the presenting client, as a means of rewarding the referrer.

When a referral comes through some more formal avenue then expectations occur again. A doctor may 'trust' the therapist with a patient but with that trust may well come an expectation that he/she will support a medical model of treatment for depression further than the therapist may actually be willing to go. This happened recently when a depressed patient expressed surprise and anger when I began to point out the secondary gains arising from his depression, one of which was weeks away from work where there lay all manner of unresolved issues concerning his authority, masculinity and potency as an individual and as a man. A switch from a female to a male 'manager' had precipitated a 'breakdown'. His neurotic anxieties had been converted into an illness and as Freud (1975) says, he had experienced a 'flight into illness'. I asked him to support me in asking his GP to change his medication. The amitryptiline which he was taking, in its full therapeutic dosage, was reducing his response to therapy to such an extent that it was becoming almost impossible to work fruitfully at all. I am very glad to say the GP was most cooperative. This client then came to accept and work with my challenges to his state of mind and emotion and soon began to talk about what would happen when he returned to the workplace; importantly, he began to link these speculations with his general state of mind and his feelings about key relationships in his life, including his past female manager, his current female GP and his loved/hated mother and distant father.

Sometimes the GP will send a patient along when intervention is almost certainly going to be totally ineffective, at least in the short term. This usually is a case of when everything else has been tried. Two cases come to mind. A very well off businesswoman rang me for an appointment after being given my telephone number by a GP. She came to discuss her fear of flying and what could be done to help her. 'When do you intend to fly next?', I asked, thinking, at the back of my mind, of a possible clinical psychology referral I could make. ' In ten days time', she replied. My heart sank. We then went on to discuss and explore the issue further. Her husband, also wealthy and successful in business, was planning a big trip to America that would involve not only a transatlantic crossing but a number of internal flights in the United States. All this to celebrate a wedding anniversary! Yes, he knew about her phobia but would not take it seriously. In addition they had a large family of young adults who all wanted to go on holiday with them, at his expense. The only member of the family 'on her side' in this matter was the youngest child, a teenage girl in her last year at school. So what was to be done? My client would not consider long-term therapy. She regarded herself as perfectly well balanced and sane, she just hated flying. Also the issue was an immediate one. The doctor had offered some drugs to take the edge off the actual experience of being on the plane. But she was angry at the attitude of her husband and family who simply pooh-poohed the problem.

After three individual sessions I decided on a radical approach to the problem and asked her if she would meet in my consulting room with me and all her family members, including two young women who were engaged to her eldest sons. This made a total of seven of them and me, who in due course assembled in my consulting room. When they arrived the room was empty. I had placed enough small chairs in the entrance hall, and said to them as they came through the door, 'Organize the seats yourselves, I will join you in a moment'. And I did. The layout of the chairs immediately confirmed the alliances in the family. My client and her youngest daughter were on one side of the room facing the rest and there was clear space between them and the rest of the family. The family had quite spontaneously, unconsciously, sculpted the situation of the family in its oedipal dynamics (Feasey, 1996). I adjusted my seating position in order to be somewhere between the contending parties and the 'battle' began.

Looking back I sometimes wonder if I did the right thing, took the right tack with them or if a more subtle approach would have been more appropriate — or would I have done better by not seeing her at all? I invited her to come back into therapy but she never contacted me again and thus left me to struggle with my doubts and fantasies about bad and good outcomes for her and the family. I took these issues to my supervisor and did as much as I could to explore my dilemmas. An important feature of this referral for me was the fact that it came from a GP practice that is friendly to psychotherapy, counselling and psychological treatment. In seeing her and arranging the family session I was to some extent acting on behalf of the family doctor. She was asking me for help for her patient and I was responding as best as I could. I concluded this case with a letter to the doctor suggesting the patient should at some time see a clinical psychologist who might help with the management of her problem. As far as the revealed family dynamics was concerned I felt it was up to the woman client to initiate any intervention on her own behalf.

All I could hope for from this meeting was an open recognition between all the parties of the emotional realities of the situation. A few weeks later she flew with the family to America and with her she took the knowledge that the whole family would have to recognize the situation that had been created between them.

After reflection I had to make an effort to initiate what I am describing as a piece of radical therapy — radical inasmuch as I used a family meeting, a kind of unconscious dramatization, risking open confrontation between family members. The challenge of this approach was to my 'normal' analytic method and stance. I had to free myself from the habit and custom of the talking therapy and the assumptions of my everyday practice. A few weeks ago a counsellor, whom I supervise, told me she had invited a young woman student to try to express her anger and despair through art. In the individual counselling sessions this young person presented as emotionally flat and impersonal in her description of traumatic events. The girl took up the suggestion and worked at home in her flat, in a very private way. She did not, however, bring the pictures to the next counselling session but talked about how releasing the experience had been. She was grateful for the suggestion. I think that there is a good possibility that she will shortly bring her 'homework' to the counsellor to share her experience of creative therapy. Experience of 'creative therapy' through drama, movement, writing and arts activities is an increasing presence in psychotherapy. It is difficult to assess its efficacy in any scientific way and for the most part we have to rest upon the appreciative statements made by clients and our own personal experience to validate its use.

A psychotherapist or counsellor may need to refer to the client's doctor. This usually occurs when a client is in need of psychotropic support. This is a rare occurrence but not unknown in my practice. The case I have in mind was that of a young married engineer who was in the grip of the most distressing and permanent depression that I have ever attempted to treat. We worked together for about six months without any appreciable relief of his symptoms. He found this distressing. I found myself becoming filled with feelings of inadequacy, totally at a loss as to how to relieve the symptoms and bring this man to ordinary unhappiness from his unreasonable misery. I finally approached the subject of medical help with him. He was at first resistant, interpreting my move as a wish to be rid of him. I struggled in supervision with this thought but I was finally encouraged to pursue the point and he eventually progressed from me to his GP and then to hospitalization. Frankly I was relieved, as I thought his life to be at risk.

This takes me to the issue of making judgements in the assessment process. The medical model insists upon looking for a treatable disorder, giving it a name and an understood programme of treatment with an expectation of outcome that to a large extent can be predicted. But as far as psychotherapy and counselling are concerned it is a different story. A referral coming from a medical colleague will inevitably be coloured by traditional notions of diagnosis, prognosis and cure. Certainly some conditions can be recognized quickly in their more florid presentation. Here I am thinking of depression or anxiety. But these too may be quite heavily disguised on a first therapeutic meeting, or may not be what they seem. In the following vignette the client entertains as a means of defence against the encroaching despair.

John came to my therapy room dramatizing himself much in the manner of Woody Allen in one of his more neurotic, self-regarding film parts. He claimed all-controlling anxiety in virtually all aspects of his life! He described with relish and much amusement many humiliating experiences he had suffered, especially in his dealings with women. I found myself grinning and very much wanting to join in his tales in a competitive way, especially as I had recently seen *Annie Hall* and thoroughly enjoyed it. He truly was a seductive client. But why was he with me and what was he seeking? At another level I found myself puzzled and confused. It was many weeks before the defences shifted, the disguised material began to emerge in the therapy room in a more genuine manner and the therapeutic relationship became less manipulated.

A number of clients seeking counselling present as if just a short talk will deal with their problem. And of course sometimes it does. The task of the counsellor is very much to learn to listen, but to listen with insight and to the dialogue that is enacted rather than spoken. Much of John's communication was in the body language: the slumped shoulders, the sad face, the worried eyes, the nervous hands, the rigid back, his legs tangled and tense. Often a referral to the counsellor has arisen as much from the unspoken language of the body as the apparent presenting problem spoken about to the doctor. I suppose the most dramatic example of this is the young woman or man suffering from anorexia nervosa, where the physical statement is open and demanding and the spoken statement sometimes hidden, evasive and misleading. Obesity can be equally powerful in its message, although is rarely received with any sympathy. In John's case he was the lead actor in his life drama and to feel fulfilled and appreciated: he needed an audience. So he performed, entertained, amused and paradoxically distracted attention from the pain of his condition.

Behind this discussion of referrals lies a more complex issue, which is the manner employed in assessment and the principles on which it is based. Psychoanalytic literature has been full of this topic. Counsellors too may be interested to consider the place of assessment in counselling and the way in which analysts have wrestled with the problem. Psychotherapists and counsellors encounter clients from a range of class and intellectual backgrounds. Some appear more suitable than others for therapy, more likely to gain benefit than others. This notion immediately brings in its wake the question of how we make our judgements and how this affects our assessment procedure as well as our practice. Here I would like to quote from an article I wrote on this subject published in *Changes*, Vol.16, No. 2:

It is generally known that Sigmund Freud's patients and the subjects of his case studies were on the whole female and without exception middle class, some of them very intelligent and well educated. A good number of his patients in the later period of his practice would be analysts seeking a training therapy. In most cases they were from a professional background. Freud himself did not seem to think it of any significance or interest that these were middle-class patients, many of them sharing a common class cultural background. Certainly he does not write about them in those terms. In his *Introductory Lectures in Psychoanalysis* Freud (1976) persistently describes his patients in the most generalized of terms, employing the adjective 'neurotic' to distinguish them from those he describes as 'normal'.

The subject of class hardly seems to enter his consideration. This does not surprise me. Even in our present time one can hardly imagine most psychoanalysts giving much consideration to the issue of class in their experience of private practice. Geoffrey Gorer, a social anthropologist, in a sharp and incisive essay in *Psychoanalysis Observed* (1968), comments with barely concealed irritation on the absence of 'cultural' understanding in the theories and practice of 20th century psychoanalysts. He is particularly scathing of Melanie Klein, the founder of what is sometimes described as the 'British School'. He notes that in Kleinian therapy it would appear that the notion of a patient having a valid or influential cultural experience upon which to draw as a contribution towards the therapy is of no importance. Furthermore the cost of private analytic therapy is usually well beyond the means of working-class people. Freud seems never to have considered the problem. For analytic psychotherapists working in the public sector of mental health, however, it is a quite different story, although rationing of access and therapy time via the waiting list is the usual situation here. But I feel sure for many public service counsellors and psychotherapists money and culture will be a significant question to be resolved, hopefully in favour of the patient.

However, Freud *was* interested in what he described as 'external resistances', and he gives the subject some attention in his lecture 'Analytic Therapy'. He writes: ' many attempts at treatment miscarried during the early period of analysis because they ... were undertaken in cases which were unsuited to our procedure and which we should exclude today.....' In this instance he does not identify what he would consider unsuitable characteristics in a patient at the time he gave the lecture but he does go on to describe what he calls 'unfavourable external conditions'. In this instance he is referring to the family of a patient who 'stick their noses into the field of operation', and he goes on to ask: 'how can one ward off these external resistances?'. He is very pessimistic about the possibility of dealing adequately with this situation and goes on to quote a case where a husband intervened and looked on the analytic procedure with 'disfavour' because he realized his 'own catalogue of sins will be brought to light'. In the light of what I have just presented of Freud's thinking I should in all fairness quote him, again from the same source, when he writes: 'You will guess, of course, how much the prospects of treatment are determined by the patient`s social milieu and the cultural level of his family'. Here I think Freud is using the term 'cultural' in an evaluative sense, not in a more modern sociological sense. What Freud describes as the social milieu and cultural level would now probably be interpreted as characteristic of class and education.

Freud mentions another objection that is generally accepted in psychiatry as being contra-indicative for psychotherapy. Patients suffering from acute psychotic delusions are generally felt to be unsuitable for analytic psychotherapy or counselling because they cannot exercise 'insight' into their delusional system. Storr (1979), whose work I shall be considering at a later stage, states on the issue of patients suffering from delusional paranoia and other psychotic states that 'they should not be treated by the beginner psychotherapist'. Storr was writing before counsellors were on the scene. It is difficult to quarrel with this view but it speaks more of the limitations of the therapist than the unsuitability of the client!

The issue of suitability comes up quite forcefully in *Individual Psychotherapy in Britain* (editor Windy Dryden) and a number of contributors refer to selection as a problem and an area where the therapist needs to show skill in predicting likely outcomes. Dryden himself, in the introductory chapter of this book, refers to contributors such as Fransella and Inskipp who write about the issue of over-dependency in potential clients. Dryden refers to Mackay, who worries about the threat of intimacy to some clients when drawn into the closeness of a dyadic relationship with the therapist; he also speaks of Faye Page, who believes that 'highly manipulative' patients may do better in groups than in the closer relationship offered in individual work. Such patients are sometimes described as 'borderline patients'. The list continues: there are those who over-intellectualize (Collinson, ibid.), then there are those with sex problems, which appears to be the concern of John Davis and may contra-indicate individual therapy. Finally there are those highly skilful clients who find the individual therapeutic relationship too 'comfortable'. This reminds me of an occasion when working in Hungary. I was asked by the director of a residential community therapy centre how I had fared with a staff workshop, and I replied that I had found the analytical staff the most 'difficult' to work with. He replied blandly, 'Of course, they are most experienced in defence'. But aren't we all — including the readers of this article. Reading the list of reservations in Dryden's list, one begins to wonder who *are* the right people to become clients? One cannot help wondering whether, as a profession, psychotherapists put their own conceptualization of the 'right kind' of client before almost everything else in their thinking when selecting clients. In the Dryden volume, Cassie Cooper puts this forward quite clearly; she writes: 'The Kleinian therapist would see himself as working best with a patient whose underlying conflicts were towards the narcissistic side; whose ego had undergone considerable deformation or weakening... '.

Thus we see potential patients being classified into specific limited qualifying categories, following almost a medical model of specialized need and consequent treatment by specialist consultants. One can imagine a situation where such categorization could lead, in a fantasy scenario, to the following: 'Having had my narcissistic wounds treated by a clever Kleinian, and thankfully they are healed, I can now pay attention to my defective super ego. So I will seek a referral in that direction. A Freudian of the independent school should do the trick!'.

But a much broader category of patients may be disallowed: those who are described as only capable of 'concrete thinking' and attempt to resolve problems through action. They are said to 'act out'. But to my mind this is a simplistic division. All of us, to some extent or another depending upon the particular circumstances of our lives, 'act out' and/or reflect with insight upon our dilemma, whatever that might be. Usually, to bring about change we 'act' in some way or another and our reflection on the action and consequent 'insight' might guide us in the right healthy direction — as Foulkes puts it, 'into a state of equilibrium' (Foulkes and Anthony, 1973) — or it might not; I do not believe that therapists are in any special privileged position in this respect. We have to approach with caution the notion of persons who think concretely and act, rather than reflect, as being unsuitable for psychotherapy. These persons are, for the most part, identified as working class in origin, of low educational attainment and regarded as not likely to exercise reflection and insight in the conduct of their lives. (Feasey, 1998)

Since writing the article I have had a confirming experience from a 'working-class' man who is just leaving therapy. He talks with great sensitivity about the manner in which he has become accustomed to reflecting and thinking and talking about his feelings, thoughts and relationships. He came to therapy two years ago quite naively and sceptically. My experience has been that the client soon reveals whether he/she can and wishes to work in a psychotherapeutic mode. The *learning* component of psychotherapy and counselling needs stressing. The client may take a little while to get the hang of the unusual relationship offered by either counsellor or psychotherapist. But if the professional handles the situation with care and respect, leading the client sensitively to embark upon and use the therapeutic relationship, then only a few clients will fail to stay the course. He/she will learn, as we have learned in our profession, how to do it. Just by coincidence, as I write this chapter, I am being invited to attend a meeting of the British Association of Group Psychotherapists to consider what they describe as the controversy of assessment and consequent selection of clients for psychotherapy. Clearly this is a contemporary issue. If I attend it I shall be talking about psychotherapy as a learning experience, for client and therapist alike.

Chapter 5
Appointments

Anyone who goes to a psychiatrist ought to have his head examined.
(Sam Goldwyn. Quoted in Pepper, 1985)

It is only natural that we should judge the success of our practice, especially private practice, by the number of appointments that fill our appointment book. I have already pointed out that I struggle with either a famine or a flood. Both states bring problems. When I worked in the NHS, in a specialist psychotherapy unit, the flow of referrals was watched with some anxiety by us all. Too few meant that we were being ostracized or neglected by psychiatrists who could have sent us 'suitable' clients. On the other hand, if we had too many we knew we could cope only with a known number of patients. Putting people on a waiting list was no answer to their pressing needs for psychotherapy. Indeed it could easily have lead to disillusion.

In private practice the therapist/counsellor is at greater risk. Working as a single-handed practitioner can be a difficult position to maintain when the referrals do not come or do not come in sufficient quantity to sustain the counsellor/therapist, either economically or psychologically. Our personal view of our value as counsellors or therapists is to a large extent determined by how we are valued by others; professionals who refer to us confirm our sense of worth, clients who come self-referred similarly confirm for us our value as counsellors/psychotherapists and of course as worthwhile human beings. So appointments stand as a central concern for therapists and counsellors whether working in the NHS or in private practice.

For the counsellor/therapist in private practice the telephone is the key instrument in initiating and confirming the psychotherapeutic appointment. The question then arises: who answers the telephone when a client rings? In my household the only permanently resident persons are me and my wife. We are both well practised in answering the telephone to potential clients. If I am engaged when the telephone rings and my wife is available she simply tells the person to ring again and suggests a suitable time. She avoids any discussion of the practicalities of my availability. And that is about it. Of course, on rare occasions, she has to field more demanding telephone calls. But these are rare and she is skilled at managing the situation as it arises. If we shared our household with many other people this could be a problem. Imagine an eager six-year-old taking an appointment call for mummy or daddy! An answering machine picks up the calls when I am in session and in my recorded message I offer to ring back in the case of an enquiry, which I always do when the person leaves a request and contact number.

Talking recently to a colleague he confessed he was about to have another telephone line installed with a separate number for his counselling enquiries and clients. His family found the access his potential and current clients had to him and to them, via the telephone, intrusive and disturbing. My feeling about this issue is that the economics of my practice would have to be very good for me to go to such lengths. Obviously having a telephone/answering machine in the therapy room is to be avoided.

I find managing the appointment system more tricky than I ever imagined it would be. Part of the trouble was that I turned away from the classical arrangement in psychotherapy where the clients are seen at the same time on the same day throughout the therapy. This was partly for practical reasons and to suit me as well as my clients. I will not work in the evening or at weekends and so my clients find ways of seeing me at other times. As a result I feel an obligation to meet their contingencies of time. There is more rearrangement of appointments through the week than I think really desirable. What follows is that there are more times to go wrong, and they do, more often than I would like. On very rare occasions I have faced the horror of two clients arriving within minutes of each other, although fortunately not actually on the doorstep, jostling one another for priority. The first to arrive was the one with the properly confirmed appointment who was seen, and I was left with the excruciatingly difficult task of turning the other away. For an analytic therapist the internal psychic repercussions of this situation are complicated and painful, although I am sure it would have been equally confusing and disturbing to a counsellor.

Before leaving the matter of appointments there is a need to deal with this in respect of fees. Should missed appointments be paid for, and if so, in full? What special conditions should be laid down to protect the missed hour from financial loss, and what kind of notice should be required if the client rings to change an arrangement? Some counsellors and therapists 'bill' their clients monthly by invoice or ask them to pay for blocks of time. Different practitioners will answer these questions according to their own circumstances. There cannot be an absolute ruling. As far as I am concerned I reduce the fee by half for an appointment cancelled with twenty-four hours' notice. If the notice is less then I require full payment. If an appointment is successfully changed to a different time and day in the week in which it should take place, I do not penalize the client in any way. As far as the deserting client leaving me with an unpaid bill is concerned, my practice is to follow up with a couple of letters of enquiry and a request for payment. If there is no response I drop the matter.

What must also be addressed is the fact that the manipulation of appointments has psychological meaning and clients often express both their dependency and distance from the counsellor or therapist by their attendance or absence from the consulting room. Recently I was quite shocked, annoyed and disconcerted when a client, a United Kingdom Council for Psychotherapy registered therapist, missed an appointment, made no contact with me, ignored my follow-up letter and did not pay my fee! He should have known better. The telephone call is often the boundary between the counsellor/therapist and the client; it is also the interface. This space is for the most part clearly understood by clients and is rarely abused in my experience. However, problems arise. What is the correct response to anxious third parties? A mother rang me from London concerning her student son who was in therapy with me. I was reticent and guarded in my response, pointing out my obligation of confidentiality towards my clients. 'But', she insisted, 'all I want to know is whether he is keeping his appointments with you OK; surely you can tell me that?'. A few days later I had a telephone call, again from London, this time from a psychiatrist, well known in the field for his publications, acting on behalf of this same mother, asking much the same questions. We are faced with these confusing incidents from time to time and it is better to appear to be rather rigid than find yourself manoeuvred into a breach of confidentiality, which could put the therapeutic relationship at risk.

It is quite common for relatives to ring me to make an appointment on behalf of someone they care for and feel very worried about. I know it must prove immensely frustrating to them when I reply that I need the person concerned to telephone me to make an appointment. I cannot contact the potential client to initiate therapy. Even when a person is in therapy with me, I hesitate to discuss or change appointments through a third person. The client I mentioned, who has abandoned me and not paid my fee, instructed his secretary to ring me and cancel the first appointment. The promise made was that my client would then follow up and ring me for a further appointment. This never happened. The depersonalized cancellation call was indicative of what then followed. The therapeutic relationship was 'rubbished' and I was forgotten, overlooked, without explanation.

In response to early enquiries I tell potential clients that I will be glad to meet them for an assessment appointment. I explain that it presents an opportunity for them to meet me and get the feel of what I might be like to work with. At the assessment meeting they can make any enquiries they wish concerning the conditions of therapy and how I work. Also they can express their needs and I can respond to them, and they can form some opinion as to my suitability as a psychotherapist. Obviously I am assessing the client and deciding whether I can profitably work with this person, to see if we are going to 'fit' one another. As has already been discussed, suitability for psychotherapy is quite an issue in the analytic world. I rarely hear counsellors discuss the issue, which does not mean that they always find all clients easy to deal with or that they do not feel more at ease with one client than another. Very recently I had a supervisee counsellor complaining about the lack of psychological insight displayed by her client. Some clients, although intelligent and committed to work in counselling or therapy, can appear psychologically or emotionally unresponsive. A mother recently expressed astonishment to me that her two young sons cried to see their father, after a miserably conflictual divorce, when access to the children was at first denied to him. She seemed quite unaware of the vulnerability of the children and her manipulative control of their relationship with their father. There were echoes of this behaviour in the history of her own paternal relationship, which she had experienced as persecutory, controlling and depriving. In these circumstances the patience of both counsellors and therapists is strained as we are put so painfully in touch with the pathology of our clients and, perhaps, our own failures to be the best parent or the most cherished child.

As far as the clients are concerned, I think most of them are looking for evidence of empathy and concern in the therapist/counsellor during the assessment session. This is a subjective experience, much of it initially in the unconscious, soon coming to consciousness and influencing the client as he/she comes to a decision. The assessment interview in private practice, must, unlike its NHS counterpart, deal with practical issues of money. I always tell clients as they enquire that there will be an assessment fee. At present it is £20. However, this is my minimum fee and I expect to negotiate a higher fee with the client if his/her financial circumstances support this. I also provide a formal written statement of my professional registration for the client, naming the institute of which I am a founding member: the West Midlands Institute for Psychotherapy and registration with the United Kingdom Council for Psychotherapy. Clients then have some evidence of my competence and the ethical character of my position. Oddly enough, in the NHS, it is completely unusual for a professional to provide such information. Indeed a client may think he/she is being treated by a fully qualified therapist/counsellor when in fact he/she is being seen by a trainee who is being supervised. This is a common practice. Much worse is the situation that arises when a nurse, psychologist, occupational therapist or social worker may offer counselling when they have received no specific training in the theory and methodology of counselling and are relying on peripheral training experience during their own training period.

When I worked sessionally in an NHS mental hospital I sometimes did assessments on the ward. On these occasions patients often assumed I was a doctor. I made it a matter of principle to ensure they knew I was a non-medical psychotherapist and if they did not wish the interview to go forward then there was no need for it to do so. Many therapy and counselling centres in the NHS or in university counselling services use honorary therapist/counsellors who are in training, anxious to get experience and accumulate training hours. I am not against such practice. It is within the tradition of psychoanalysis, counselling and medicine. I felt fortunate that a consultant psychotherapist was willing to let me work alongside her in her NHS practice during my own training period. On the other hand, I do think the client should be informed of the situation and given a say in the matter, better still a choice. Everything that informs the client should be available when it comes to making a choice of therapist/counsellor. The client should not be misinformed. We should remember that withholding information is a way of encouraging disinformation. For example, whilst it is obviously a sign of high intelligence and effort for a therapist or counsellor to have gained a PhD of a non-medical character, I think it is misleading, in the context of NHS or private practice, for a therapist to use the title 'Dr'. To have it recorded on an answering machine or stencilled on a consulting room door is entirely misleading. The obvious deduction for most clients, coming to what they may imagine to be a medical experience, is that the therapist is medically qualified, a psychiatrist specializing in psychotherapy. I now notice there is a disturbing tendency for some clinical psychologists to use their academic doctorates in the same kind of way. Presumably it is more about status and rivalry than a concern to inform the client of competence.

Thus the assessment appointment is by its nature different in kind and quality from the usual therapy interview. I think most therapists and counsellors will use the opportunity to test out the ability of the client to speculate, to interpret for him/herself and to show a creative curiosity concerning his/her difficulties. In the assessment chapter I talked of psychotherapy and counselling as a learning process and the qualities mentioned here are part of that process. At a more subjective level, as counsellors or therapists we are monitoring ourselves during an assessment interview to get the feel of the client and to discover if the seeds of a good working alliance are present. At a rather extreme level, if the therapist or counsellor feels an instinctive deep dislike of the client, then it is unlikely that the relationship is going to be productive. It would probably mean that the therapist would have to spend too much time in supervision, sorting out the rational and objective from the irrational and subjective, to be of much use to the client. In my own practice I have monitored the assessment interviews from time to time and discovered that approximately one in four leads to a stable, continuing therapeutic relationship.

The counsellor or therapist working for an institution, of whatever character, usually has a working day bounded by contract. Most will work a nine-to-five day, have paid holidays and sick leave. They may even be fortunate enough to be included in a pension scheme. In the following chapter I shall discuss finance in more depth but here I need to consider the way in which appointments structure the day for the private practitioner. At a mundane level I constantly frustrate myself and my friends when replying to invitations by saying, 'I cannot say anything until I get home and look at the appointment book'. My day, my working life and social life are controlled very largely by the appointments I have during the week. This is a fact of life, a necessary condition of being a therapist or counsellor in private practice.

Is it possible to keep appointments to the framework of a working day? Drawing on my own experience the answer is yes, although undoubtedly it has cost me some clients but not a large number. I remember this being an issue from the early days of my practice when I was hungry for clients, both for the sake of experience and for the fees that I needed to earn. I was fortunate, living in a small university town, that the first clients I had recommended to me were from the university and they were able to come during the working day. However, gradually, as I became better known, I received referrals from people busy in their professions and businesses where time off from work to attend therapy sessions is at a premium. This was a problem. I stuck to my guns then, as I still do, and work only from the earliest appointment at 8.30 a.m. through to 5.15 p.m., finishing at 6.15 p.m. There is, naturally, a pressure on the late appointments and I have had clients who have always attended before going to work. Being someone who enjoys a lie-in, I find the latter irksome but not impossible. My only concession to the work patterns of others is to offer a flexible lunchtime appointment; sometimes this helps them. It does not often arise but it is there to be used where it can be helpful. My experience is that, after initial dismay at restricted availability, the client soon settles down to an appointment ritual and is remarkably faithful to the contract. Therapeutically there is a lot to be said for the conservative rituals of regular, same time meetings. A relationship develops in this way and underpins the trust and openness required if there is going to be a good outcome for the client and the therapist/counsellor. More often than not when a therapeutic relationship fails, there has been a great difficulty in keeping appointments and sticking to a regular regime of attendance. Often the counsellor/therapist struggles too long with a client who is constantly changing dates, times or cancelling at the last moment. Analytic psychotherapists know the safe approach to this phenomenon is to interpret, within the therapeutic context, what is happening and perhaps to steer the client towards a safe finishing point, closing the therapy. Although this may be known, sometimes the therapist is confused, lacking insight and the relationship struggles on in a somewhat muddled way. In my experience of counselling supervision this has been evident there too, and sometimes it is almost predictable from the first that the relationship with the client is not going to survive. The counsellor concerned may be distressed and anxious, even angry at this apparent failure, but as the old saying goes, 'You can take a horse to water...' etc. Nothing is truer than this observation. The failure to 'drink' may be inherent in the relationship with the therapist/counsellor and may be a symptom to be dealt with in the therapy, but sometimes it is just a way of saying, 'look, this is not for me' or 'you are not the one for me'. Sometimes it is up to the therapist to call off an appointment. Recently one of my most severely physically disabled clients rang me, much concerned. He was feeling ill. He had pain in his body. He could not get an appointment with his doctor until a time when he had an appointment with me the next day. We discussed the matter on the phone, but I was quite clear in my own mind that he really needed to see his GP and my appointment should not get in the way. The dilemma for him was that his time with me was on a Friday. If he did not come on that day, at that time, he would have to wait another week to see me. He lived at some distance and an arrangement for him to make up the lost appointment by coming twice in a week was not practicable. So I had to advise him to see the GP and delay his appointment with me for another week.

Appointments are important. Attendance at appointments, on a regular basis, is the essence of good therapy and counselling but like every other truism sometimes the rule has to be overruled. Regularity and order must not become punitive rigidity. My view is that psychoanalytic therapists are more likely than counsellors to find themselves imprisoned within an inflexible way of working. A final question on this subject: How many appointments should a counsellor or therapist keep in any one day? It is difficult to answer this one. I regard four appointments a day as my usual full allocation and on rare occasions I will keep five. In the latter case it is usually when I see one person for supervision and the remaining four for therapy. In the end it must be decided by the individual and it will necessarily be determined by subjective factors such as stamina and the desire to be productive in the work; of course, money also comes into this — the need to earn enough to pay the gas bill.

As human beings, counsellors and therapists are no different in their basic needs than others. We need to be creative in our lives and loves and for that we need time and resources. The appointment book frames our professional existence and is indicative of the needs of others. But it can be argued that benefit to our clients rests upon our ability to remain good human beings, balanced in harmony in our lives, including our working time. To that end the appointment book needs to find its proper place in the larger structure of our lives.

Chapter 6
Money

He that has nothing but merit to support him is in a fair way to starve. (Anon. in *Characters and Observations*, early 18th century. Quoted in Pepper, 1985)
Nothing is intrinsically valuable; the value of everything is attributed to it from outside the thing itself, by people. (John Barth in *The Floating Opera*. Random Press, 1972)

[The analyst must not treat money matters] with the same inconsistency, prudishness and hypocrisy [with which] civilised people [treat].......sexual matters. (Freud in *On Beginning the Treatment*, 1913. Quoted in Reichman, 1950)

In this chapter I shall be concerned not only with the practical issues of fees and earnings and expenses but also with the symbolic meaning of money and how it is variously interpreted in our society. Freud, of course, openly and readily interpreted the presence of money in our psychic lives and much of what he wrote and interpreted remains of interest to this day. The debate goes on. Those who have read Ernest Jones's (1964) biography of Freud will know that Freud struggled with practical money issues all his life and was constantly in debt to others who supported him. He rationalized this situation by claiming that the loans and gifts were evidence of how much he was valued by colleagues (Freud, 1974). A neat one! He also worked long hours to support his family whilst at the same time producing scholarly works upon which his professional work is based. Professor Carl Rogers, although a renowned psychotherapist, was first and foremost an academic psychologist and his income will probably have come largely from a salary and publishing. He appears to have had little to say about money. Indeed, the index of his definitive work, *On Becoming a Person*, makes no reference to money. Strange for one coming from the land and culture foremost in capitalistic values.

Perhaps the issue of money and its importance and meaning in our lives represents the last taboo. It is noticeable that in chat programmes on television virtually every aspect of human existence can be raised and discussed with talk show guests, other than money. The presenter/host can probe into the most intimate areas of a guest's sexual life and personal relationships but will studiously avoid asking 'How much do you earn?'. If such a question should be put there is usually a frisson of anxiety in the studio audience response. I was for some time on the highest governing council of a 'new' university. This was some twenty years ago. There had been a succession of professorial appointments made by an academic appointments committee but it seemed impossible to find out what these new professors were being paid. So I raised the matter at the council meeting in the form of an enquiry to the Vice-Chancellor. The result was an embarrassed silence. Most of the rest of the council, about a dozen or so men, many of them top businessmen, avoided eye contact with me. It was as if I had suddenly started to use swear words and obscenities in my question to the Vice-Chancellor. As an experienced university politician he managed to avoid answering the question, whilst suggesting I had asked an indelicate question which no sensible person would dream of asking. What a crass person I was, he implied; how indelicate and blundering I had shown myself to be.

Interestingly, in the present age, the same situation is mirrored in the secrecy of special merit payments made to consultant psychiatrists in the NHS. I have never been at a meeting where anyone, including me, has had enough courage to raise the question. I have been in many staff groups where *other* emotional issues, especially of destructive envy, have been addressed with a show of frankness and openness, but the issue of money has been avoided. It rather looks as if Freud was right when he compared money to excreta, a material we regard with secret pleasure and disgust. A woman who has a well-paid job in education, where equal pay has been the rule for many years, was talking to me about giving up her full-time job in favour of part-time work and then making up any financial deficit by working as a counsellor, possibly in a GP practice. I restrained myself from observing a rather dry, 'You should be so lucky!'. A quick survey among counsellors who do work in GP practices tells me that the financial rewards are modest. A counsellor can expect to be paid somewhere around £15 per hour. This does not sound too bad until it is realized that the counselling hours are not that many. In addition I have come across cases where patients have been offered less than an hour of counselling in order that the hard-pressed counsellor, working to a limited number of hours in a week, could see as many patients as possible. There is usually no security of tenure, no holiday pay, no sick pay or pension provision. The counsellors concerned are effectively self-employed. There does not appear as yet to be a nationally agreed rate for counsellors working in clinical psychology services or in medical settings, although a number of counsellors are now actively attempting to get national agreement on fees to be paid to counsellors in GP practices and other medical settings. Two organizations come to mind: the Counsellors in Medical Settings and the Association of Counsellors and Psychotherapists in Primary Care are active in pursuing the question of fees and conditions of service for counsellors and psychotherapists. An enquiry to a number of departments of clinical psychology showed that counsellors were paid much less than psychologists. I discovered two large departments where the counsellors were paid on a scale related to a clerical administrative post. I found this really shocking and felt angry towards the departments for paying such a miserable rate and, perhaps, even more angry towards the counsellors for accepting such payment. Two other large clinical psychology departments did not answer my enquiries and I am still waiting for them to ring me back! There is a money culture in psychotherapy and counselling as there is in virtually all employment. It appears that it is difficult in the counselling world to organize the counsellors, working as they do in a fragmented milieu, but the situation is changing and it now seems that determined efforts are being made to rectify the situation.

There is a scale for adult and child psychotherapy operating in most hospitals and a newly qualified psychotherapist, at the bottom of the scale, could be expected to earn about £18 000 per year where a permanent contract exists. This scale goes back to a time when analysts in London were being encouraged to work with children in specialist centres, and originated some thirty years ago. We can be grateful to the psychoanalysts, who had some idea of their own worth. Nothing is settled or publicly spoken of in the field of private counselling and therapy. There is an underground, rarely explicit, rate for the job in individual psychotherapy, group therapy and supervision, as well as special rates for consultations. The latter is still very unstable and I had an instance of this recently. I was asked by a supervisee to nominate a therapist who could act as an independent consultant in an advisory role to a hospital authority. I did so. Much later, when the subject came up again, I was amazed to learn that the therapist I had recommended had charged hundreds of pounds for the expertise she offered the hospital. I was shocked and regretted my recommendation. Similarly, I was asked by a colleague to suggest a psychiatrist who would do a private assessment of the psychotropic medication being taken by a client. I did so. The client went to the psychiatrist I had named, waited patiently in a busy NHS clinic for an interview, and the appropriateness of the original GP prescription was then confirmed. The meeting lasted about 15 minutes and the client was sent a bill for £150. I deeply regretted giving the referral. I shall be more careful and reticent in my future recommendations. I shall certainly ask about the money involved.

My own practice is to provide enquirers with a printed statement of my range of fees for individual psychotherapy, couples work, group work and supervision, either individual or group. At present my smallest individual fee is £18 per hour and the highest £40 per hour. The sum is arrived at through discussion and according to my client's means, needs and frequency of attendance. If a client comes more than once a week I work out a weekly fee, with the client, that client feels he/she can afford and maintain.

The fact is that the training of counsellors and psychotherapists grows more and more expensive almost day by day. Apart from the academic training costs, the personal individual and group therapy and supervision required of trainee therapists is increasingly expensive. Masson (1992) speaks sharply of the problem of training costs. He was attending therapy five times a week and talks about 'a substantial part of monthly salary went to pay for analysis'. Later on he looks at the question of investment. 'Admitting failure would have been costly on all fronts: for my self-esteem, for my professional career, for my personal life and my finances'. Fees charged reflect the overall growing costs of training, as qualified therapists and counsellors try to recoup the costs of their own training. Sometimes this situation is described as 'fleas on the back of fleas upon the back of fleas...etc'. I can offer a little comfort. It seems that the Inland Revenue does, in some cases, allow the cost of initial training to be set off against income tax liability. This relates to course fees. I think it is possible that they might allow the cost of supervision and training therapy. The situation is of circular escalating costs that feed back towards the clients. Janet Malcolm (1982) in her excellent book writes about the analyst Aaron Green (a pseudonym) complaining bitterly about his lack of riches and his envy for those analysts who are rich. Most of them would be traininganalysts, high in the hierarchy of their training institutes. He complains too of the client who owed him money for some eight months and states ruefully: 'And I allowed it to happen ... one of the most heroic things I have ever done as an analyst'. Unlike many therapists he is disarmingly frank about the place of money in his professional life.

But training costs are certainly not the only financial burden falling upon the counsellor/therapist preparing for and in private practice. There are the hidden costs, that is, hidden from the client, of providing a place to meet, furnishing it appropriately, keeping it pleasantly warm in winter and cool in summer. The costs in capital equipment of such a room are considerable. Good quality durable furniture and carpeting are expensive. Heating and lighting do not come cheaply. The space has to be cleaned and kept in good decorative order. Another approach is not to provide any of these facilities at home but to rent rooms in a therapy centre. These centres are now becoming increasingly available. However, this in turn represents a cost in monetary terms and sometimes there are distinct practical disadvantages to the use of such premises, bearing in mind that you as the tenant do not have the last word on how the centre is organized and who else uses it.

It is likely, too, that the therapist/counsellor will want some office space and office equipment. I am typing this on an expensive computer with a word-processing programme. I also find I increasingly use the e-mail service and fax and pay the rental of a telephone that also connects me to the Internet, and I own an answering machine. Mind you, I am not a minimalist. I can think of a counsellor colleague who disdains most of these props and makes only one concession to the world of technology: she owns an answering machine. So it is up to the individual to decide how far to go down the road of communications technology.

Before turning to the psychological aspects of money and its place in the therapeutic relationship it is sensible to address some other practical issues involved in earning and spending. If the therapist or counsellor decides to become a self-employed person all sorts of benefits and charges then accrue. The main benefits come in various tax allowances for providing and equipping a workplace, running a car, going to conferences and attending courses. But, and it is a big but, remember tax benefits are only available if you are actually earning significant sums of money. My luxury is to employ an accountant to help me present my accounts every year and to pursue any tax benefits on my behalf. But do not think this takes away the responsibility of preparing an income and expenditure statement. The grind has to be done and this means keeping records of fees and payments of all kinds, where you are lucky enough to earn them. Tediously, too, it is necessary to keep receipts and records of allowable expenditure which will include such items as stationery, telephone calls, travel, conferences and seminars, membership of professional bodies, professional insurance, purchase of books and journals. Capital items are furniture and equipment, such as a computer, filing cabinets and office equipment. My accountant earns his fees, not only by keeping my accounts in order and me on the right side of the law, but by finding every advantage he can for me in the business of legitimate expenses. Thus from time to time I get agreeable tax rebates for which I am duly grateful. My accountant was useful and helpful in drawing my attention to the need for and the advantage to be gained from a private pension fund. He put me in touch with a financial adviser who, fortunately, was a man of integrity and knowledge, and pointed me in the right direction for a pension fund provider. I saved with this company for some 15 years and now I have bought an annuity that supplements my occupational pension and my state pension. This is all very satisfactory. However, I have found a number of counsellor women friends and colleagues seem to have a curious blindness when it comes to making sensible financial provision for retirement, or at least retirement age. I will resist a generalized psychoanalytic interpretation, believing that to make one is futile. I cannot account for this reluctance to face reality except in sexist terms, which will probably infuriate some readers of this book. I wonder if the ageing process is even more uncomfortable to women than to men. I do not think anyone particularly relishes the process and I certainly had to overcome resistance in myself to putting aside money for a questionable future!

One particular irksome outcome of being self-employed is having no one other than yourself to subsidize further training, except through a tax break. I miss the days when a beneficent employer would offer me a sum of money every year from which I could pay for attendance at conferences, seminars or meet the fees of any further academic or professional training I might undertake. As things stand I have to pay everything myself and then claim a percentage against earnings.

The other expenditure I might have overlooked, were I not reminded to meet it by my professional body, is insurance to protect me from claims of malpractice. The reader might say, 'Well, I'm never going to offend in such a way'. All I can say to that is that just as beauty is in the eye of the beholder, so is the question of malpractice. Of course there is a reality to malpractice and in the last few years there have been a number of exposés of therapists and counsellors who have exploited and abused their clients. Often the abuse has been sexual, but sometimes it has been more subtle and the abuse has been in the area of money, power, influence or neglect. In Chapter 4 I spoke of the client who committed suicide. I did not expect this to happen and was very shocked by the incident. His partner, a sophisticated and intelligent woman, was very angry at his death and came to see me seething with despair and anger. She turned all her anger towards his employer. I knew the employer had behaved very considerately and humanely towards her partner and was not to blame for his death. But at another level I was thankful she did not turn her anger towards me. She might well have thought, in her distress, that I had failed as his therapist and reasoned I should be 'punished' by taking a legal action against me for this 'failure'. I would have been glad of my professional insurance with the Psychologists' Protection Society.

Now let me turn to another aspect of money. Money in the therapeutic relationship is loaded with meaning. Freud wrote with much feeling about money and its place in the human psyche: its associations with faeces; our tendency to hoard or spend freely. We speak of people being anal, retentive, holding on and holding back. Others are described as being 'fools with their money': they spend freely and without good purpose. Recently a client spoke of being seduced, by the offer of large earnings, into work which he did not want to do, in circumstances that were not agreeable to him. He pulled out of the arrangement at the last moment and, typically of the seduced figure, turned his anger towards the seducer. We all

remember the story of Midas and his dreadful fate when he received the
gift whereby everything he touched turned to gold, with its awful consequences. How he longed to escape his predicament and could not. As
counsellors and therapists, if we are in private practice we cannot fail to
notice how money enters our relationship with our clients. As John Barth
in *The Floating Opera* states: 'value is attributed'. Thus in the private
practice of counsellors and therapists the value of the skills of the therapist
is recognized tangibly by the client paying a fee. Value is then attributed.

Why do I ask for *cash*? Mostly I am concerned with the money being a
salutary reminder of the therapeutic relationship. We live in a time when
cash transactions are disappearing from our lives. We pay for all sorts of
services by credit card, direct debit, switch and cheque. We receive money
by direct credit. There is much avoidance of the place of money in our
lives and much of the time financial transactions have the character of
fantasy. Consequently I believe that to encourage the exchange of notes
and coins at the end of the therapy session is to place both the therapist
and client in a tension that illuminates the relationship.

There is an old saying, 'Money can't buy you love'. Indeed, in the therapeutic relationship it sometimes buys hate and aggression. Tillett (1998)
discusses this with some feeling when he acknowledges that he found a
conspicuous absence of this experience in textbooks he read, and the
seminars and case discussions he attended as a practising psychotherapist.
He is as much concerned with the aggression of the therapist as of the
client. These tensions are illustrated in the following accounts. Alan, a
well-paid academic, is resentful that my 'love' for him has to be bought,
and the money — paid each week, in cash — is a bitter reminder of the
truth of the situation and his own difficulties in admitting ties of love or
concern to those about him and within his family. He reacts with a show of
aggression. He is very interested in counselling and once remarked
bitterly: 'No counsellor works like this'. I notice that a number of counsellors I supervise really do not like to acknowledge that I am paid in ready
money for my services. I recall a psychoanalyst once describing the fifty-
minute analytic hour as forty-five minutes of love and five minutes of hate:
when it needed to be paid for. Paradoxically Alan values private practice
because he wants to be treated with respect. He was admitted to a private
hospital for a short stay and physical treatment, and on his return to
therapy I attempted to address the issue with him. He became angry and
accused me of irrelevance: 'I don't come here to discuss the merits of
BUPA!'. He shouted angrily. I asked him what else he would like to discuss.
He could not think of anything! Paradoxically, the same client values
private practice where he expects to be treated with respect. Again value is
attributed. He has tales of contempt about getting treatment in the NHS
where he 'was just a number', merely described as a collection of

symptoms. He felt as if the treatment was aggressively punitive. All too frequently patients in the NHS are described as 'depressives', 'psychopaths', 'personality disorders', 'manic depressives' and so on.

Another client, at the end of the session, would put the fee silently on the mantelpiece, without comment. It was always exactly right and I had no need to give any change. One day she laughed, crying out impishly, 'My God, it's like leaving money on the mantelpiece for a prostitute!'. The connection with paying for and receiving intimate, uninterrupted attention is obvious. But it is sometimes harder to acknowledge the barely concealed aggression; momentarily I was compared to the despised prostitute A highly placed professional accountant client wanted to pay me by standing order or direct debit; anything to avoid touching the money and placing it in my hands. Money as dirt, filth, excreta. Another man, a professional academic of some standing, never had any cash with him and would give me a cheque which often 'bounced'. He waited patiently for me to reject him in an aggressive manner. He spent a lot of money on prostitutes, who demanded and got cash. His 'id' impulses had to be assuaged along with a search for unthreatening intimacy with its implied aggressive penetration of hated women. His relationship with me, incorporating much of his super ego, had to be denied.

I value all these experiences with my clients and I would not like to substitute a regime where I simply sent a monthly bill to my clients or left it in an envelope, on the hall-stand, to be collected. I would regard such behaviour as one of avoidance, 'acting out' on both my part and that of the client in collusion with me. The late Nina Coltart (1993) discusses the issue of money with frank directness, but even she confesses to distancing herself from the issue of cash in case the client thinks she is merely a tax dodger. She obviously hated to be thought of as such a person and might well have hated a person who did think of her in that manner. A colleague of Freud, Freda Fromm-Reichmann (1950) states in her book that Freud advised that 'An analyst should not be ashamed to charge substantial fees, that he should collect regularly and that he shouldn't take free clients on the grounds that free treatment increases some neurotics' resistances.... The absence of the regulating effects offered by payment of a fee to the doctor makes ... the whole relationship removed from the real world ... the patient is deprived of a strong motive for endeavouring to bring the treatment to an end'. Notice Freud does not allow for the ability of the client to pay! Neither is he concerned with the symbolic meaning of the transaction. He is severely practical. For the counsellor or therapist working in the NHS or a private clinic the rich meaning of these encounters is lost, which I think is a pity, a loss for both the therapist and client. On the other hand I know that many of my colleagues become angry at what they see as the discrimination that comes into play when services have to be paid for by the client. I can go a long way with them, but at the back of my mind is that old American saying, 'There is no such thing as a free lunch'. The problem with an apparently free service is: what becomes of the value attributed to it? This question cannot easily be answered. Perhaps the answer is that the attribution lies in the position of power that the therapist holds. The 'purchaser' client may become not the 'purchaser' but the 'supplicant'. The therapist is then drawn into a position of imbalance in the therapeutic relationship. Thomas Szasz (1998) has a good deal to say about this in an article in the *British Journal of Psychotherapy*, entitled 'Discretion as power: in the situation called "Psychotherapy"'. To summarize his discussion in his own words, 'I use the term psychotherapy as the name of a freely contracted relationship between two competent and responsible adults, one *paying* [emphasis added] the other for assisting him, by means of a dialogue, to live his life better'. He distinguishes such a voluntary arrangement from what may occur when the arrangement is less than voluntary and where psychotherapy is practised within a framework that could be described as 'coercive'. The latter may occur when other agencies such as the family or other institutions of society express a 'need for controlling the Other'. The implication is that psychotherapists, especially those working in the public sector, may willy-nilly be drawn into such a coercive arrangement where the power balance between therapist and client is distorted in favour of *other* interests, note not the 'Other' mentioned by Szasz. The very worst example of this, in my experience, was the psychiatric abuse of dissidents in the former Soviet Union. But our psychiatric departments are not exempt from paler shades of abuse and the psychotherapist and counsellor have to be careful not to be drawn into this trap.

Chapter 7
Beyond the consulting room

Leisure is time at personal risk.
(A.M.Sullivan in *The Three Dimensional Man*. Quoted in Pepper, 1985)

Yes, believe it or not, there is life beyond the consulting room. Indeed it can be rich and varied and I am talking about you, the therapist, not your client. Life in the consulting room can be fascinating and absorbing, certainly, but undoubtedly enclosing, restrictive and exclusive. We all need a change. Sometimes we need *re-creation*, that is to build ourselves anew. But sometimes we simply need to find leisure and company, in the various guises of our friends and colleagues. In this chapter I shall be dealing with both the re-creative aspects of the life of a psychotherapist/counsellor, in the sense of another life outside the professional concerns of therapy, *and* the ways in which we can get a measure of refreshment in dialogue with our professional colleagues in different settings.

I will start with the second and come back to the first. Let me address the thorny matter of the supervision of other counsellors and therapists, both those 'in training' and qualified and experienced practitioners. It is deeply embedded within the culture of psychotherapy and counsellor training and practice. I have referred to it earlier as the phenomenon of 'fleas on the back of fleas on the back of...etc....etc.' and there is some truth in the observation. I announced rather proudly to a counsellor friend of mine that I had been offered a lucrative supervision contract taking responsibility for a group of counsellors; I was very pleased with myself. Without a trace of humour or irony she immediately said 'Sounds good Don, *who* is going to be *your supervisor*?'. So I riposted, 'Oh, Jane will do it... at least she *will* when *she* is able to find a suitable *supervisor*!', the implication being that she needed someone to supervise her supervision of me. And so on and so on. Where does it end?

For the therapist and counsellor in private practice the situation of supervision is subtly different than for those working in some kind of institutional setting. The therapist or counsellor in a hospital or clinic may well be clinically supervised by a senior figure in the institution. This gives rise to problems concerning authority, role and control. Furthermore, insensitive management procedures may well impact upon the counsellor or therapist, which become acute and need to be addressed in supervision. For example I once worked as a sessional psychotherapist in an NHS hospital and never succeeded in getting a secure room of my own to work in. I left. Informal supervision outside the hospital with colleagues helped me to leave and acknowledge that I was not going to win an unequal struggle. Needless to say I did not get any supervision in the hospital. I did not get any management either!

But for the self-employed psychotherapist or counsellor the situation is quite different. The institutional anxiety met with in the hospital or clinic setting is usually absent. Sometimes, where rooms are rented, problems of landlord/tenant relationship may arise. Often the behaviour of other users can cause concern. Recently a counsellor in supervision with me moaned about the rented room she uses in a local therapy centre: 'Oh', she exclaimed, 'the loos are awful, cobwebs and filth!'.

Working therapists and counsellors often have a regular supervisor that they see on a monthly basis and may continue to do so for many years. They pay fees for this service, somewhere around the figure of £30 per session. On the other hand, it is a usual activity for therapists and counsellors to offer as well as receive supervision within the culture of their practice and then supervision is a source of income, one balancing the other. I will not go into a discussion of the nature of supervision as against therapy except to say that sometimes, in my experience, it has been sought when it would have been more appropriate for the therapist concerned to seek therapy. A very experienced and well-trained psychoanalytic psychotherapist approached me recently for a series of supervision sessions to, as he put it, 'clear up old problems I have with my parents that sometimes enter into my work as a therapist'. We struggled for a few sessions to identify clearly the nature of these proposed sessions and what kind of relationship was being proposed between us. I eventually managed to define a therapeutic relationship with him that was vested in therapy and not in supervision and we began to work together, but it was not easy.

Another way of receiving supervision is to seek it with a trusted therapist on an *ad hoc* or occasional basis. I have been approached and worked with both counsellors and therapists in this way, where we have met for a series of consultations which may continue for a couple of months or so, or it might even be a one-off experience. I do not believe there are any rules in this matter; it is for the therapist concerned to decide whether to take on such work. In my view it will depend largely on the nature of the person seeking such assistance and the circumstances surrounding it.

My own experience as a supervisee has been a mixed one. For many years I had what might be described as a punitive supervisor and I often wondered why I stayed with him, and I have wrestled with the question in therapy. Even now, some years later, I still tend to idealize that person although I know quite well I am supporting an illusion! I have found supervision in a group very useful and I have enjoyed the intervention of peers in the group as well as the reflections of the group supervisor. I would advocate this arrangement but I would counsel caution at the idea of dispensing with the professional supervisor in the group altogether. Peer group supervision on a sharing basis at first seems attractive but, inevitably, difficult, even critical issues, may be avoided for the sake of the harmony of the group. It can be important for money to be exchanged between supervisees and supervisor for the service, in order to distance and control the boundaries of the relationship, much as it does in therapy.

Before leaving my own experience I do acknowledge that for a long time I received supervision from a most able and sensitive supervisor who always managed to combine a sharp and illuminating intelligence with a friendly and supportive manner. I remain indebted. This contact with a colleague or colleagues outside the consulting room is, in my view, most beneficial. Yes, there is a serious professional purpose and sometimes it can almost be like a moment in therapy, but on the whole it is more relaxed, less structured, less formal and more openly friendly than the experience of being a client in therapy. Supervision, at its best, is nearer to a relationship of professional equality and friendship than therapy can ever be and in that sense provides a truly re-creative opportunity for the counsellor or therapist.

In this section of this chapter the matter of personal therapy or counselling needs some attention. Freud thought that psychoanalysts should seek to renew personal therapy from time to time in order to deal with residual neurotic elements in themselves that were likely to interfere with their practice as analysts. For practising psychotherapists and counsellors, in the present day, the issues are not so likely to focus upon the specifically neurotic elements of the personality but rather on psychic and life events that make powerful demands upon us as human beings. I cannot think of a single friend, colleague or relative who has not at some time struggled with personal issues of the most painful and intrusive character. It stands to reason that psychotherapists and counsellors will enjoy no exemption from the traumas of life, and the fact that they are constantly exposed to the deeply felt and distorted expressions of pain in their clients' lives makes it imperative that they see to their own psychological needs and well-being. The timing and frequency of such therapy or counselling is a matter for the individual but it should not be seen as an admission of weakness, rather a resource that is at hand to support the therapist/counsellor in his/her professional and personal life. It should be borne in mind, however, that finding a therapist or counsellor you feel you can work with, with confidence, is sometimes a tricky issue.

Some time ago I felt I wanted to be in therapy again and I began to look around for a therapist. The problem was that I was acquainted with most of them and as far as I was concerned that ruled them out. I wanted anonymity and confidentiality, clear and safely boundaried. Having worked in this part of the North West of England for so many years it was difficult to find what I was looking for. I did, eventually, thanks to the United Kingdom Council for Psychotherapy register but it was difficult.

It had taken me a long time to admit my need for therapy and I was dismayed that it took me a long time to find the right therapist. Fortunately the idea of going back into therapy is usually accepted by analytic psychotherapists; it is a reflection of their training culture. I am rather concerned that counsellors sometimes, reflecting their own training experience, find it difficult to accept the notion of becoming the 'client' again. Difficult as it is, sometimes, to accept our vulnerability I believe it is a necessity to do so. So this is an experience beyond the consulting room which, from time to time, may need to be drawn upon in order to sustain and protect the therapist and counsellor. The role reversal is refreshing and the feeling of being held in a secure therapeutic relationship is renewing

With the boot on the other foot the fact that I am an independent therapist, working in a geographical area where one particular training body is dominant, has proved useful to some professionals wanting a secure therapeutic alliance where there is no boundary confusion or clash of loyalties. Independent counsellors and therapists can offer this position and it is a valuable one, but sometimes it is regarded with suspicion by training organizations that want personal therapy or counselling, for their trainees, to follow an exclusive training culture. This is especially true of psychoanalytical training where the tradition of the training therapy is a powerful one.

A more informal and less 'pathological' setting in the quest for refreshment is to be found in the 'interest group'. I feel grateful for the fact that I have been a member of an interest group in psychotherapy for many years. When it first formed, many years ago, it was a very difficult group to enjoy. It appeared to be riddled with anxiety, competition and rivalry, obsessed with issues of status and control. For a short time it was so awful that I stopped attending. I had other concerns as well. Being in a minority of almost one, as a self-employed 'independent' therapist, I often sensed a covert hostility to my private practice from some of the therapists present, who, for the most part, worked either for social services or the NHS. This broke out, once, in an openly hostile and powerful attack upon me and my private status, at a group meeting led by a senior NHS psychotherapist. I was not present to defend myself. When I heard about it I took prompt action to confront the person concerned and eventually got an apology from her. She finally admitted to me that she had had therapy with a private psychotherapist during her own period of training.

Nevertheless I persisted in my membership of the group and over the years it has changed. Its relatively exclusive 'analytic' culture has changed and now we are a more pluralistic group, welcoming therapists and counsellors from different theoretical approaches who come together and share their views and experience with a group of like-minded people. Our like-mindedness consists of a genuine interest in each other and our different ways of working. We are largely self-sufficient, presenting papers or workshops to the group on a regular basis and discussing topics of common interest as they arise. When we come across someone outside our ranks who interests us, we invite them to join us for a session and do a presentation. Fundamentally we celebrate the differences between our therapeutic practices and theories. Meeting friendly, supportive colleagues often relieves problems of isolation that may be encountered by counsellors or therapists working single-handed either in private or public practice. The humour and freshness that we can all encounter and enjoy in such a meeting puts our work in perspective and acts as a welcome relief to the seriousness with which we normally inhabit our professional lives. We can safely try out ideas and views in such a setting, especially when we are, perhaps, preparing a more formal lecture or paper for publication. It is, too, an invaluable source of referral for us when we need to find a therapist or counsellor for a friend, colleague or relative, where our own participation as a therapist would not be appropriate. The usual boundaries of relationships, which we have to exercise in our relationship with clients, can be relaxed in the framework of an interest group, although care must be taken to protect our clients from inadvertent revelation. I recall Fay Weldon, the novelist and feminist, complaining bitterly at the exchange of gossip about patients which she witnessed occurring after she gave a talk to a group of therapists in London. This happened when they all went for a drink together after the meeting. That does not mean that in our interest group we never gossip about or tease each other, because we do, often to our mutual benefit. We tend, as a profession, to be a somewhat over-serious group of people and like all human beings we need the occasional safety valve of humour to lighten our lives. But I am satisfied that we do not betray our clients' trust.

Another way of broadening our professional lives and refreshing our personal selves is to attend seminars, workshops and conferences. Clearly there is an educational aspect to these visits and we should remember that new learning is a way of refreshing ourselves and keeping at bay a tendency to rely upon received established ideas to which we are all prone. Both counsellors and psychotherapists tend to be, in my experience, over-attached to the basic ideas that were imbued during their training, which is hardly surprising. Obviously, we will go to workshops that attract us. But counsellors and therapists, especially those who are well established, would be well advised to deliberately seek out that which is challenging, new or radical. Given that the training of counsellors and psychotherapists tends towards the passive, that is sitting, listening and talking, it can be enormously refreshing simply to expose oneself to therapies that encourage action and contact. One of the most enjoyable and authoritative workshops I have ever attended was with an aromatherapist, which took me somewhat by surprise. Perhaps age comes into this discussion. A young colleague argued recently that the 'oldies', such as myself, seemed broad minded and receptive, tolerant of approaches to psychotherapy and counselling other than their own. It was the younger graduates who appeared to be the most rigid and orthodox.

I have trained and qualified as a dramatherapist and psychodramatist. Psychodrama, in particular, emerges in action as one of the most effective diagnostic ways of working I have ever discovered. Through role-play and role reversal, doubling and sharing, most participants are brought rapidly in touch with the central areas of concern in their lives. A simple example is in the following anecdote, from a time when I was conducting a psychodrama session in a therapeutic community. Each patient was, during the months of treatment, encouraged to work through a session of psychodrama. At this session, Julie was preparing to examine, through drama, the current relationship with her parents with whom at the age of 44 she was still living. We started with a discussion and I then invited her to choose a place where she might meet her mother and father. She chose the sitting/television room at her home and began, without any assistance from me, or the co-director or the patient group, to set up the furniture in the remembered, imagined room. She placed two armchairs in front of the television set, put in place a coffee table and stood back.

'Is that all?', I asked. 'Yes', she replied. I heard a gasp from someone in the patient group who was watching but for the moment I decided to leave Julie to examine the 'set'. She looked baffled. Then she moved one of the armchairs nearer to the TV set. 'Dad likes to sit quite close', she observed. 'And mother?', I asked. She moved to the other chair and shifted it marginally. There was a mounting tension in the room and one of the observing patients began to move towards the scene. I guessed what was coming and let him advance. He went and stood beside Julie. I said, 'Julie, Robert is going to double for you' (to 'double' is simply to speak for the client, as if in the voice of the client, stating possible thoughts, conscious or unconscious). Julie was familiar with the technique and merely nodded. Robert went closer, touched her shoulder and said 'There is no room here for me, I shouldn't push in and try to get between them'. In that moment, in one simple sentence, Robert touched an emotional nerve-end. Julie went pale and looked pleadingly at me. 'Yes?' — I put a strong questioning inflexion into my voice, giving her a chance to reject the interpretation. In a small voice she muttered inaudibly, and then louder, 'Yes, it's true, there isn't, I'd be better off somewhere else. There's no place for me here'. The classic oedipal struggle of the triadic relationship between child, mother and father had been recognized. The psychodrama continued in the form of action and dialogue and ended in reflection that was remorseful and purposive within the group.

I give this example simply to show what can be achieved through allowing into our possibilities of therapy and counselling alternative approaches. Going to workshops and seminars where we encounter the new, opening ourselves up to novel and unexpected approaches, can be a source of great renewal. As a psychoanalytical therapist I have always recognized that the unconscious reveals itself in action, as did Freud (1974), of course, in his book *The Psychopathology of Everyday Life*. In the instance I have given, the client simply 'forgot herself' when she set up the scene, forgetting to put out a chair for herself, perhaps revealing the wish that she wanted to be out of the scene. And yet she was 'in it', too closely perhaps, when there was not sufficient room for her, in an emotional sense, in her parents' relationship. Her oedipal struggle over the years to displace her mother had been in vain, and now in the drama was a moment of recognition.

I have heard colleagues express a cynicism, which I do not share, about the motives of conference attenders. A friendly counsellor went halfway round the world to sit in the shadow of a guru. He came back entranced and renewed. Some counsellors and therapists go to 'network', to get themselves seen by and known to persons they imagine might have power and influence in the matter of jobs and referrals. My response to this suggestion is that we cannot, with any certainty, know the motives of anyone other than ourselves, and then only dimly. And of course, in all of us is a desire for recognition and love from those we may admire. I am not so shocked or judgemental in this area as some others might be. I suppose I am willing to admit foolishness in that respect, in myself and others, with a degree of forgiveness.

It has been said to me, by a good friend, that being a psychotherapist is to experience a social handicap. I agree with her: I think that that observation is to some degree true. In Chapter 3 I referred to my problem as a partygoer; now imagine the following scene: a small sophisticated Italian restaurant. The tables are very close together, the waiters attentive, perhaps a shade too much so. We have all enjoyed the meal, some good wine and the buzzy atmosphere of the restaurant; now our conversation flows freely, we have become rather disinhibited and at some point as my wife is in deep conversation with the woman friend I make some passing reference to masculinity to my old friend. He explodes. Suddenly he is shouting at me, quite incoherently, making all kinds of explicit sexual references both verbal and gestural, which now the whole of this little restaurant shares with us in a mixture of curiosity, annoyance and scandalized pleasure. This is becoming quite an evening! I manage to calm him down and the tumult subsides. His woman friend is remarkably undisturbed; she maintains a poised air of loving concern towards him and some minutes later when we are all doing our best to contain and restore the feeling of the evening she turns to me and says very quietly, 'Don, you are in a dangerous profession'.

To be a psychotherapist is undoubtedly to place yourself at some social disadvantage. I find myself avoiding telling people what I do when being introduced at social gatherings and I am quite adept at doing so. But of course relatives and friends do know what you do and this can intrude into your relationship with them, as it did in the restaurant story. The family may come to expect too much of you as a father, mother, brother or sister, uncle or aunt or whatever. The therapist is supposed to be an expert in human relationships and therefore is always sensitive to the needs of others, is always thoughtful and kind, always understands the difficulties of other people's lives and is always strong and supportive. Well, what a lot of bunkum this all is. As Shylock said in the *Merchant of Venice*: 'If you prick us do we not bleed?' As a profession, we are especially susceptible to these projections towards us and we may, on occasions, allow them if we experience these expectations in a flattering, demanding or powerful way.

Some time ago I became depressed at the loss of an important member of the family. I had all the classic symptoms of depression: sleep disturbance, irritability with those around me, loss of energy and a feeling of loss of interest in the social world around me, a preoccupation with my inner self and a lack of interest in those close to me, and an all-consuming anger towards what had occurred. I was grieving. My family had to cope with all of this and I also felt a kind of shameful guilt that I was imposing on them a state of being that a psychotherapist ought to be able to deal with! Of course, this is nonsense: I needed help. As I related in the previous chapter, to the relief of those closest to me I sought help from my doctor and another therapist.

Most fatally we may try to practise therapy on ourselves or our loved ones and thus create a fatal distortion in our personal relationships within our family culture. I have never succumbed to this temptation, although sometimes therapists come under considerable pressure to work with a relative of close friends. This may be tempting and seem possible but the only sensible advice to give here is don't!

A more subtle situation arose when a friend of our family became very depressed and had to 'go sick'. She was off work for weeks and after some time asked me to recommend a therapist, which I did. Unfortunately the referral was not a happy one. After some months our friend said she could not keep going to the therapist any longer. It appeared the therapist was, in the opinion of our friend, not addressing the most important core issues in her life and spoke of her as being too fragile to work in depth. Would I find her another therapist? I did. But the internal repercussions of this issue have lingered in me. It is absurd. I know the feelings are irrational but the truth is that I became too involved in the process altogether. I am sure my colleague, too, must have had quite deep feelings concerning what occurred. Sometimes the personal and professional can become blurred in our wish to be helpful and supportive to friends and colleagues.

I am conscious that this is a discussion, in part, about boundaries. It is probably true that becoming a counsellor or psychotherapist is to enter a professional world of social inhibition. The therapist working in a small town is inevitably going to encounter clients from the past and present in various situations. This phenomenon needs addressing in the therapeutic relationship. For years clients knew that if they encountered me in the street or in a shop or cinema queue I would, if they so desired, acknowledge their presence in a restrained modest gesture. We would not talk or greet one another in any way that implied a normal friendship. Occasionally the encounter with a client would occur in more intimate situations, such as being guests at a party, where the hostess did not know of our therapeutic relationship. The therapist sometimes has to make a small sacrifice of interest. I remember going one evening to join an evening class and to my dismay a particularly demanding client was in the lecture room. I had to make a decision quickly; I knew it would only ever be a small group and as students we would be required to enter into discussion where personal material would be explored. I withdrew. Working in a large city these encounters are less frequent but still on occasions take place. A young woman client sits in the cinema with her boyfriend. He puts his arm fondly around her shoulders. She wriggles away from him, quite uncharacteristically. She shifts her body away from him. The language is distancing and rejecting. He responds with a hurt glance and moves away from her. A few days later, recalling the incident, she said to me quite harshly 'You were sitting behind me, you could see everything. I felt a right fool!'. This is just another example of the social hazards of the profession of counselling and psychotherapy, which feed back into the therapy room, challenging the boundaries of therapy. Each therapist has to make up his/her own mind as to how to deal with such experiences. For some therapists and counsellors it will be more discomfiting than for others. I work in transference but that does nothing to relieve the discomfort of unplanned encounters such as I have described. It is obvious that negotiation with clients, in advance of such unplanned encounters, may be required.

The counsellor/therapist needs self-confirming experiences as much or as little as anyone else. But there is a need to be somewhat self-denying in this respect in situations other than the intimacy of one's own family. This is where conference, seminar or workshop time is valuable. To be among peers is to abandon the need to explain, or justify, or deal with the sometimes overly high or low expectations of strangers or acquaintances met with at social gatherings. Quite the contrary atmosphere often pervades meetings of therapists and counsellors where people seize the opportunity to reveal their humanity in its various aspects. This is especially true where colleagues attend workshops at which it is possible to expose, in a safe way, feelings that for the most part we inhibit.

Holidays too need to be valued, planned for, timetabled and protected from the demands of our practice. The reader may complain, 'But I have no money!'. This, sadly, may be true but the notion of the holiday is not that of expensive adventuring in foreign parts, or at least it does not need to be. The holiday should be seen as time set aside for re-creation. Literally to feed and nourish oneself in the manner that is known to be most fulfilling. This may involve money, which then needs to be saved to provide the holiday. For others, a holiday may simply be the providing of time to visit or be visited by friends. Yet another person may simply want time alone to pursue a hobby or interest, something as simple as gardening or a bit of do-it-yourself. Many counsellors and therapists use holiday time to refresh an intimate relationship. Time with a partner, husband or wife or close friend, walking together, sightseeing, bathing, resting, preparing and cooking good meals, travelling together are all ways of holidaying with a creative purpose and outcome. Last year my wife and I spent a warm, sunny afternoon walking along a high ridge on a Dorset hill near Corfe Castle. It was an emotional and physical achievement for both of us; we savoured the experience, it refreshed us and we go back to it in memory frequently. More recently we both swooned at the beautiful sound of the BBC Philharmonic Orchestra playing the Poulenc Organ Concerto. Such moments literally take you out of yourself into another dimension of being, a long way from the consulting room.

Alan Prodgers (1991) states, 'Compassion, care and concern for others, love, sympathy, a non-judgemental attitude are held in high esteem by therapists'. This description of human qualities would also apply to counsellors. These are the desired attributes of good parents, too. Many counsellors and therapists are fathers and mothers and I would like to close this section of the book by drawing attention to the needs of children in their growing-up period, and the special responsibility that falls upon us as parents, perhaps made more difficult by our professional insight and training. Children have powerful developmental needs as they grow towards maturity. For the most part psychotherapists and counsellors are only too aware of their responsibilities in this respect. It can be a burden to know that as a parent you are not quite good enough all of the time, but only some of the time. Children usually show an indifference to our professional burdens, requiring us to understand when others do not; to show tolerance and patience at virtually all times; to be emotional providers, calmly putting aside our own needs in favour of our progeny, and so on and so on! How unrealistic it seems when written down in this way. But, nevertheless, most of us with a family to nurture judge ourselves demandingly.

My view is that what children want from us throughout their lives is time and attention, even if, at times, the circumstances of both time and attention may be fraught with tension and anxiety. We provide time and attention to our clients as part of our professional expertise, exercising patience and forbearance. So much is obvious. What is not always so obvious is the way in which the job can reduce our energy so that giving emotionally to those who matter most to us becomes difficult. As the children get older, especially when reaching adolescence, they may regard our work with some amused embarrassment. How can they tell their mates what we do? Our work may make us more vulnerable to their coolly critical eye as they view our relationships with those closest to us. They may well mutter 'therapist heal thyself'. It is a scrutiny we may find difficult to bear but we must, we have no choice in the matter.

How we are seen by our clients and those around us is a matter of concern to most of us. Analytical therapists commonly cherish a kind of anonymity in their therapeutic relationships. Counsellors are, perhaps, less concerned. Recently I became involved in a political debate in a public way. The issue then becomes should I deal with this in the therapy room with my clients, perhaps drawing attention to any discomfort they may feel in not agreeing with my declared political position? Is this a transference issue, to be treated as such? I decided not to raise the matter myself, unless it became absolutely evident to me that the client was seeking a clarification and was hesitantly approaching me with the issue. There can be no absolute ruling on matters such as this; much will depend on the character of the counsellor/therapist. I have always considered myself a political citizen with a responsibility to the society in which I live and sometimes it is necessary to speak out on sensitive and pressing social and political issues, though preferably not in the consulting room!

Obviously, here we are approaching the issue of the value system of the particular therapist or counsellor. Religious as well as political feelings and beliefs play an important part in the lives of us all. This becomes apparent in the counselling and therapeutic relationship and needs to be addressed rather than denied. The idea of the therapist or counsellor being outside the value debates of society is absurd, and damaging to the humanity and integrity of the worlds of counselling and psychotherapy. The issue is how far our participation in those debates should intrude into the therapeutic relationship. I can think of occasions when I have run up against issues of race, class and sexuality in my practice as a psychotherapist and I have had to clarify in a fundamental way, first to myself and then, on rare occasions, with a client, the position I hold.

Chapter 8
Communications and confidentiality

There are no secrets except the secrets that keep themselves.
(George Bernard Shaw in *Back to Methuselah*. Oxford University Press, 1945)

When I was in the early stages of my training as a psychotherapist it was my habit to write up case notes at length. I do not regret the time and effort that I invested in this way. It was a necessary part of the training process. I would try to formulate an understanding of the client, and record as faithfully as I could the therapeutic conversation between us making note of any especially significant issues or forms of speech or silence, body language and emotional tone that accompanied the exchange. In the current situation for psychoanalytically trained therapists and, to a lesser extent, counsellors in training, there is a requirement by the training bodies for the trainees to write and present case notes including formulations and, in some instances, interpretations, upon which the therapeutic relationship is based.

However, as my practice grew this intense note taking proved impractical. Having had a good deal of psychiatric supervision in the hospital where I worked sessionally as a therapist, I was accustomed to writing lengthy notes during the first few assessment interviews with patients. Included in these notes were doodles and cartoon-type sketches I sometimes made to highlight certain topics and concerns introduced by the patient. For example, a patient might gesture toward certain parts of the body to illustrate and even dramatize an emotional state of being. Not surprisingly the heart, head and the stomach were frequently pointed to as sources of pain or 'upset'. This was all part of my continuing awareness of the body positions of patients and their non-verbal communication during interviews, so for three sessions I would make detailed recordings of the interviews and this is the habit I have brought to my private practice. After these initial sessions my notebook disappears and I write up only certain data after the session. For example, all life decisions and actions are recorded, such as a client divorcing a husband or wife, or leaving home or changing a job or going on holiday. In other words, I am concerned to record change of life circumstances. I faithfully record any changes in my contract with the client, especially concerning frequency of attendance and fees. These are often important indicators of movement and change in therapy, sometimes in a positive direction, sometimes not.

On a practical level I keep these notes in a cardboard folder, not on the computer, so that without deliberate effort my relatives and friends would not stumble across them. They are confidential documents and often contain material that is shared only between the client and me, and they are in my keeping on the understanding that no one else is going to read them. This would include all correspondence and sometimes pieces of creative writing and artwork that have been entrusted to my safe keeping. My experience in the hospital service soon disenchanted me of the idea of confidentiality within the hospital system. The reality was that once the notes were made the patient had no control over them and nurses, doctors, other health workers and secretaries could read whatever took their fancy. This sounds rather harsh but it was undoubtedly true in the hospital where I worked. In my private practice it is quite otherwise. The only person who is likely to read the notes, apart from myself, is my client.

All correspondence concerning my client between me and third parties is shown to my client and I always make this clear to all concerned. So for the client in private practice confidentiality can be real and respected. Indeed, it is of primary importance and valued as such by clients. This is not always understood by other professionals outside my practice and sometimes leads to tension when I refuse to answer enquiries without the express permission of my client; any written communication is shown to the client and agreed upon by him/her before it is transmitted anywhere else. Where trainees are involved the same ruling applies as far as I am concerned. I do not write confidential reports on trainees which they do not have sight of. I show trainees what I have written and ask them to agree, sometimes with amendment, to the report being submitted to their trainers as required. The same applies to supervisees, who sometimes ask me to act as a referee for a post for which they are applying. In this circumstance an enquiring employer is told that the reference has been seen by my client. Wherever a report is required, the same principle applies. Basically I am a servant to the client, although I hold certain ethical reservations in this matter that apply to all clients and are the concern of all professional counsellors and therapists. I state quite openly that I reserve the right to break the confidentiality principle if I believe the client may be at risk of physical self-harm or placing others at such risk. Nevertheless, the working principle of confidentiality applies. A substantial article by Katherine Venier (1998) discusses this topic in some depth. She concludes that the issue is a complex one. She writes: 'Definitions are at best ambiguous and there is much confusion between privacy, anonymity and confidentiality; and what each entails and their limitations'. I noticed that in this list the word 'secret' was not mentioned, yet therapists and counsellors are all parties to keeping secrets, another deeply ambiguous and resonant term with certain pathological attachments. As therapists and counsellors, are we limited to partial confidentiality and at what point should the exception be invoked? I have stated my own position and it is up to each counsellor and therapist to decide on a position and make it clear to clients, bearing in mind the requirements of any validating body to which they may belong. Venier (1998) discusses this issue with some subtlety and with a useful survey in which she addressed questionnaires to 143 United Kingdom Council for Psychotherapy (UKCP) registered psychotherapists. I was surprised and somewhat dismayed to read that the general acceptance of the inviolability of the confidential therapeutic relationship was nowhere near as prevalent as I had imagined. Although 93% of the UKCP professionals said they would notify a client of the intention of involving another professional worker or GP, only 60% would seek permission to do so from their client before making the contact. I can only imagine a good number of these therapists work in the public sector.

Another intriguing and difficult subject is the question of the use of confidential material in case studies. Jane Polden (1998) uses the provocative title 'Publish and be damned' which, I admit, drew me to read her authoritative article on the subject of writing about clients and publishing case studies. She argues, convincingly, that the topic is endless and could lead to total inhibition on the part of psychotherapists in respect of publishing case studies, other than those about themselves! Jane Polden advocates getting the agreement by the client to the use of therapeutic material when it is to be published. Basically I agree with her but the problem of 'old' material still persists. How far back should the therapist go in trying to get that permission? Sometimes the original client has completely disappeared from the scene, and may even be dead. I have been in practice now for twenty years. In this book I have avoided anything like a full case study presentation, contenting myself with short vignettes to illustrate the principles and topics I am describing.

As to the long-term issue of notes and their use, it is well worth remembering that since the change in NHS regulations that gave patients the right to see their case notes a request may come your way for such access. In the following instance it arose because a former private client of mine was admitted to an NHS hospital as an acute psychiatric admission. The concerned doctor asked me to comment on my former client's mental health. I agreed to do so with the cooperation of my client. This agreement was given and I wrote a short summary of the condition of my former client as I had experienced him, using a mixture of psychiatric and psychoanalytic language. At the time the client did not see my report. You can imagine my surprise when the client concerned contacted me recently, some twenty years after the events, and challenged the meaning of some of the language I had used in my report. One phrase I had used was 'hysterical conversion' and my client had understood the term hysterical as an abuse word. He had frequently been accused of hysterical behaviour by practitioners in the health service and by relatives. He was shocked to come across my report using this term and saw it as a betrayal of the trust that he had placed in me. I was able to reassure him, up to a point, but it has left me feeling vulnerable and cautious when it comes to supplying information to third persons. At an intellectual level I find myself in agreement with clients having the right to read and copy any written material that exists about them in a clinical setting but sometimes the repercussions cannot be foreseen. The emotional impact of this incident, coming back to confront me twenty years after it had originally taken place, was considerable. The lesson is clear: 'look before you leap' and 'think before you write'.

About five years ago I went to a clever 'computer freak' and asked him to put together a simple but adequate computer for me so that I could write professional letters, keep records and write articles and a possible book. I had no thought of the Internet, faxes or e-mail. He did what I required for a modest sum and off I went. My computer man, although an expert in his field, was no teacher and I exasperated him with my simple enquiries and slowness of learning. More recently I gave away my old 386 and bought a Dan Computer, recommended by *Which?* magazine, that can do everything — or at least it would do if I knew how. The Dan advisory service has been excellent at listening to my simplistic enquiries with patience and understanding. Only one adviser, losing patience, told me to buy a book on word processing: I did.

Confidentiality of psychotherapy practice is an area of potential irritation for relatives of the therapist. Generally speaking, the private therapist can offer a degree of confidentiality to clients that is largely missing in the NHS or, for that matter, in the increasingly fashionable private hospitals and clinics. No secretary or receptionist gets between the therapist and the client and I have a habit of always ringing back a client who is trying to get me on the telephone when I am otherwise engaged. I handle all the records myself and no one else gets to look at them. I have already stated that I was quite shocked when I first worked sessionally in the NHS to see different members of staff getting out confidential files and reading them without as much as a 'by your leave'. I find many clients come to me because they want confidentiality and privacy in a form that cannot be replicated in the 'public' hospital or clinic, NHS or otherwise. Throughout this section of the book I have been using the term therapist but the basic principles apply to counsellors and indeed to anyone working in this area of human need.

At one time the words 'fax' and 'e-mail' were to me just jargon. Now I have eagerly embraced both through the medium of my PC. I correspond with other professional colleagues and organizations by email and fax, although I find that e-mail is much the more satisfying of the processes. The effect of this is to strengthen contacts and relationships and it enables the solitary therapist to communicate with the world outside economically and swiftly. There are, too, the so-called Web sites where the therapist can find like-minded persons discussing and exchanging ideas about therapy. The UKCP has a Web site: www.psychotherapy.org.uk.

Clinically, I have, in one instance, found the fax facility a boon. A profoundly deaf client wanting to telephone me would instead send me a fax to which I could respond. Of course it is quite possible for a beginning therapist to manage a practice without any of these facilities; I did so for years. There is no doubt, however, about both the usefulness and pleasure, even entertainment value, of the modern PC equipped with a modem, the modem simply being the box that makes it possible for your PC to communicate through fax and e-mail. At first it all appears a formidable learning experience but once mastered the PC pays real dividends. However, Katherine Venier (1998) utters words of warning. The Data Protection Act (1984), The Access to Personal Files Act (1987) and the Access to Health Records Act (1990), whilst affording patients' rights certain protection do not, in themselves, address the issue of digital and electronic transmission. These acts are concerned with paper-based records. With e-mail it is now quite easy to transmit documents anywhere in the world, very cheaply, at the touch of a button. Furthermore information can be disseminated instantly, concurrently, to as many other e-mail readers as may be required by the sender. In addition it should be borne in mind that once data has been transmitted the author has no further control of its dissemination. If an e-mail entry code is known to a number of persons in an organization, its library of texts can easily be opened and read. What, then, of confidentiality? Therapists and counsellors are confronted with more and more ethical dilemmas as digital, worldwide communications grow increasingly sophisticated and become available to the general public. For more information, contact the Data Protection Registrar, Wycliffe House, Water Lane, Wilmslow SK9 5AF. Tel: 01625 545 745.

A man recently suffered the loss of his wife after some thirty years of marriage. She went off with her lover. After she had gone he spent hours trawling through her computer searching for damning evidence of her infidelity and, interestingly enough, her financial activities. He was convinced that he would find evidence of fraud and financial deception as a kind of accompaniment to her sexual betrayal. He found nothing of this character but it made me shudder. I tried to imagine circumstances in which someone might trawl through my hard disk, summoning up files to satisfy a voyeuristic desire which, of course, is in all of us. Years ago, as a senior academic, I used to secretly enjoy my skill at reading documents left lying on the desks of my superiors, although they were upside down to my view. I could do it without strain and enjoyed this minor delinquency. The urge to see and know what is forbidden or secret is difficult to resist. I had a friend who regularly babysat for neighbours and told me confidentially that she loved to read through the bits and pieces of information that her neighbours left carelessly lying around. One evening she had a particularly good read when she came across a recently drafted will: an intriguing document. Of course, voyeurism ranges from the most innocent and playful experiences of childhood exhibitionism, which Stafford Clark (1975) discusses and describes, through to the far more complicated sexual activities of adulthood that Freud would probably have called perversions.

How do therapists and counsellors recognize when confidentiality becomes secrecy? Psychoanalytically trained therapists are encouraged to challenge clients and address their defences and this may be done in quite an open confrontational way. Sometimes the issue is one of secrecy where the client is nursing a destructive secret that may, in certain circumstances, be shared with another secret person. The obvious example here is in the instance of sexual, emotional or physical abuse in the family. For counsellors the situation is very different but whatever technique they are employing they know that secrets and resistances are present in their counselling relationship with clients. However, it can be argued that simply the presence of the counsellor in the relationship with the client is a challenge to the presence of the destructive secret. As trust and communication develop in the counselling relationship so the deadly secret is challenged. In both psychotherapy and counselling there is an element of confession that is quite appropriate. Getting something 'off one's chest' is often, in itself, a cathartic experience. Of course, when it happens, the scenario changes and yet subtly remains the same because now the deadly secret is subject to the rule of confidentiality and remains a new kind of secret. This happened when a woman confessed to me that years ago, whilst on an adventure holiday travelling alone through the Middle East, she had been befriended by a man who helped her in all sorts of practical ways but then, after a drunken evening together, raped her. She felt both angry with the man and ashamed of the rape which, in part, she attributed to her own sexual behaviour, drunkenness and naïvety. The difference, for this young woman, was that she had now spoken to a powerful 'therapeutic figure' of father-like character and as a consequence felt a measure of relief in so doing. She could not at this time in her life confess to her parents and receive their blessing, forgiveness and concern; on the contrary, she had no confidence in their ability to suffer the disillusion that the information would have brought to the family relationships. So what became a matter of confidentiality inside the therapeutic relationship remained a deadly secret in the family. It was a changed situation because at least now the information and the experience of keeping the secret, and its significance, could be addressed in therapy.

We have to protect our clients from breaches of confidentiality both in our everyday life within our social settings and more formally in our professional lives, working and communicating with other professionals. The general rule is not to disclose without permission, sometimes spoken sometimes written, but this is very difficult to achieve in reality. I like to write and teach and this book is an example of the dilemma that then confronts the therapist, counsellor/writer/teacher. Where the client I wish to describe, within a clinical setting, is currently 'in therapy', then usually no problem arises; the client either gives permission or does not. However, frequently they are figures from the past. Virtually all the clients quoted in this book are such figures. What then? My way of dealing with the situation, while sticking to the truth of the material I am illustrating, is to disguise the client so that the chances of recognition are pretty negligible. This can be done by changing the place and time of the events and so on. Sometimes this is impossible. When that is so, the advice must be not to use the illustration, to abandon it and look for another approach to the subject you wish to address. As this is being written I am aware that there is now emerging a school of thought that is looking critically at the publication of clients' confidential information in published case studies. Both Breuer and Freud (1974) were concerned about this and say so explicitly in the preface to the first edition of *Studies on Hysteria*. However, as if this is not complicated enough, we now face issues about the use of both audio and video recording, which are becoming increasingly common as instruments of training. I once worked in a clinical psychology department where a young clinical psychologist in charge of video-recording equipment insisted all tapes be wiped clean at the earliest opportunity after recording. It was sometimes awkward to meet these instructions but I eventually came to respect his diktat. Similarly, where trainees record sessions on audio- or videotape for supervision purposes, in my view the tape should be wiped clean at the end of the supervision session. Some years ago, as a psychodramatist I challenged, within the professional body, the portrayal of clinical psychodrama on public television. This caused a great stir and I was thoroughly demonized for speaking out against what I had seen as a grave breach of confidentiality. I am glad to say this abuse of confidentiality is no longer admitted as proper by the

British Association of Psychodramatists and for the most part practitioners respect this position and personal psychodramas do not appear on television

Very recently I have had to approach a client for permission to describe some problems that arise in the area of communication when the client presents a particular problem. In this instance it was profound deafness. I have never had a client presented to me before, in either my hospital or private practice, who was found to be profoundly deaf. When I was first approached I agreed to see the person concerned because I was completely intrigued and because I had not grasped the problems involved in dealing with profound deafness. After the first mutual assessment session I felt as if I should abandon the attempt to be the therapist in the relationship. I felt utterly exhausted by the effort of communicating. The client could lip-read with great skill and could speak with clarity of tone and fluency but I felt I was not a good subject for lip-reading and presented difficulties to him in that respect. Furthermore, I had not realized that there is a 'political' issue concerning lip-reading and signing as the prime method of communicating: signing is often the preferred method of communication between deaf people. The reality is that I cannot 'sign' and in any case the very act of signing has a certain dramatic character about it that normally never occurs in my everyday psychotherapy practice. My client likes signing, he enjoys its dramatic possibilities and I had to learn to enter his culture whilst at the same time maintaining my own as therapist. A small illustration will suffice to show the difficulty I sometimes experience. I try to avoid pointing at a person if I am speaking to them. Most hearing people regard that as no more than good manners. In therapy to point to a client could be regarded as a significant controlling gesture, probably pathological. I cannot imagine a sensitive Rogerian counsellor ever pointing at a client. But as I have grown more and more accustomed to the signing activity of my client, who has brought more and more of it into the therapy, I have found myself responding with my hands, arms and face. And so on occasions I point, not only to him but to myself and to particular parts of myself, for example to my ears, to my eyes, to my head, all of which are aspects of my communicating self. Working with this client has brought home to me how remote the culture of deaf and blind persons is from the world of psychotherapy and counselling. It is a learning experience and I am grateful for my client's patience and persistence in learning to work with me as I have had to with him.

Now I am aware of the fact that a similar situation exists for those who are blind, totally or in part. I am sure there are persons who work within the blind and deaf communities who offer counselling or therapy in some form or another, but the absence of such categories in my own practice is a matter of concern to me. The psychoanalytic culture does not seem to be accessible to those persons experiencing deafness or blindness or other significant impairments, for that matter. In some respects there are obvious explanations for this situation. In the case of deaf people, the emphasis on talking with the tongue and listening with our ears in our talking therapies must, at first sight, represent an almost impossible category of barrier. This could apply equally to the counselling school of therapy as well. I have great difficulty in interpreting the problem and understanding why I have no referrals for a blind person. I had an opportunity to raise this issue with a very experienced analytic psychotherapist in the NHS recently and he confessed that in over twenty years of practice he had not treated a blind person. Perhaps the thinking is that we, as therapists and counsellors, would not 'see' the problem. There is obviously an area of research here that needs attention. Why are we as therapists and counsellors failing to communicate with these persons? Those experiencing difficulties with seeing, hearing and speaking are all about us but precious few, it seems, get into the consulting room.

Before leaving the instance of the deaf client the issue of the use of the telephone immediately arises. It is very difficult to communicate to the deaf person where it is necessary to telephone to cancel or amend an appointment. I have tried using the fax to this end and it will work, but it is not my preferred way of contacting a client. There is a special telephone service for deaf people whereby a hearing operator acts as an intermediary and the deaf client communicates by typing in his/her enquiries and responses. These are then read by the operator and passed on to the hearing person on the telephone at the other end. This works well enough once the counsellor or therapist is familiar with the procedure. However, such an intermediary acts as an unwitting censor to the conversation and in these circumstances a degree of inhibition comes into play beyond the normal experience of the therapeutic relationship.

I have spoken of the culture of therapy and the culture of counselling. The lesson that is learned from encountering a client who is defined by the absence of one of the human senses is to receive a challenge to the culture with which we are familiar. Whether it be the world of psychoanalysis or person-centred counselling we need to acknowledge the fact that we move inside a professional culture that has its own language, its own special forms of behaviour and its own value system. Largely this supports the work of the counsellor or psychotherapist and is generally regarded as a good thing. Many of us have worked hard to learn the language, the forms of feeling and behaviour of our professional culture and we incorporate its value system into our being. But it has to be acknowledged too that the culture may represent our limitations, boundaries that operate in a restrictive sense, making it hard for us to connect with a culture that challenges our own. Sometimes the issue is of language, sometimes it is of technique in the conduct of a relationship but sometimes it is more threatening and we find ourselves and our professional identity powerfully threatened within a relationship in which our basic assumptions are threatened. In the psychotherapeutic relationship with the profoundly deaf client I had to face this possibility. At first I was dismayed by the tensions and adjustments we were playing out in the establishment of the relationship. The juxtaposition of the chairs in the room, the lighting levels, the body positioning were all matters of stressful adjustment and power struggle in the early days of the relationship. I had to learn that I could not communicate with him when he moved away from me and his back was turned towards me. I had to understand that when he rang the front door bell he could not hear it and he had to take it on trust that I had heard it and would come to the door — a simple assumption to which I had never given any thought before.

His big adjustment was to work with me through lip-reading, which ideologically he disliked and which aroused many feelings of anger in him, derived from both actual as well as imagined experiences of discrimination. He had presumptions about analytic work that he brought to the sessions as well as some earlier experience of counselling, and the two sometimes came into conflict. My style of working, unique as it must be, took him by surprise and challenged his stereotypes concerning psychoanalytic work. Dealing with the matter of language and what words may or may not be used in a narrative quickly became an issue. For example, the word disabled was abjured, not admitted in his cultural framework of reference and the qualities of profound deafness were celebrated almost in a sense of rivalry with that of the world of hearing. The spin-offs from these assumptions were manifold and significant and we struggled together to find words that could be used to explore a potentially explosive clash of values and assumptions. The issues here are not merely psychological or psychoanalytic: my view was that I had to address issues that were in part culturally fundamental to the world of deafness and which were not properly accounted for in my own psychoanalytical framework of reference.

As far as his body language and facial expression were concerned I grew to appreciate this aspect of his communication. As a dramatherapist it was not particularly difficult for me to accept and appreciate the dramatization he enjoyed using to emphasize a point he wished to make to me. I responded in a modified form using a wider range of gesture and facial expression than I would normally use.

Talking to a group of counsellors recently I found myself emphasizing the need for them to take into account the body positions, gestures and dress presentation of clients when counselling is in progress. The client is always communicating to the counsellor and the counsellor, whether consciously or unconsciously, is responding. The notion that, as human beings, trained in counselling or not, we can entirely control our communication signals is a fallacy. The most the counsellor can hope to achieve is a degree of self-awareness in the counselling relationship that goes beyond our normal everyday sense of a relationship. The same applies to the psychoanalytic therapist who must also contend with a tendency towards a position of absolute self-awareness in the therapeutic relationship, which can easily go unchallenged unless a supervisor is present who has a very sensitive ear for such omniscient behaviour.

The telephone and the answering machine are common features of our equipment. In earlier chapters I have referred to both. Here I just wish to state again and amplify the character of the telephone, which we all tend to take for granted. A small matter but an illustrative one is the way in which a telephone call can break through boundaries. All of us can recall an occasion sitting in an office discussing an important matter with another person when suddenly the telephone rings and immediately you lose your place in the pecking order of attention. For some years I was supervised, privately, by a skilful psychiatrist who had a special interest in psychotherapy and much sound experience. But it infuriated me that he would take calls from the outside world when I was in session with him. If I protested, he said: 'Well, I am a doctor and I am on call'. I was up against the medical culture. Masson (1992) recalls with some bitterness his training analyst taking telephone calls during therapy sessions, apparently quite indifferent to the anger of his analysand. Most of us accept the presence of the telephone without question and the priority it gets in our attention. Whatever we are doing has to stop for the telephone. Obviously this instrument should *not* be in the therapy room, although only the other day my client's mobile phone, which was in his briefcase, began ringing just as we reached the end of the session and he proceeded to have a short conversation with a business colleague!

I have referred briefly, earlier in the book, to the situation that arises when friends or relatives of the client try to contact us by telephone. This is often done with the best intentions in the world. I know that the psychoanalytic therapist is resistant to these interventions when they take place but I think counsellors are often not so protected by proscription from entering into such a dialogue. Complications arise, especially in the area of confidentiality and particularly when the client is an adolescent or young adult, such as a student at the local university. Boundaries are then threatened and the client may well lose confidence in the counsellor or therapist. It is probably necessary to quickly inform any person approaching you by telephone, supposedly on behalf of a client, that you will of necessity inform your client of the telephone call and the substance of the conversation. On the other hand, intervention from the family of the client may well indicate that there is need for family therapy. On rare occasions I have found it useful to call a family conference when a young person is involved, of course with the client's permission and active cooperation. I call to mind working with an adolescent girl who, according to her mother, 'Always told lies and worried her father to death'. After some sessions alone with this girl she eventually, rather petulantly, told me that she had been telling me a 'load of lies'. I said it did not matter very much because I was interested in *what* she said to me *not* whether what was said was literally true. She was intrigued and pleased by this response and spoke about some of her more lurid descriptions of adventures at discos and clubs as being close to dreams that she sometimes had, where she often played the 'femme fatale'. Her emerging sexuality was obvious. Eventually some sessions with the girl and her mother and father proved fruitful and the family oedipal anxiety was relieved somewhat. It is commonplace for fathers to suddenly become aware, in a most anxious way, of the burgeoning sexuality of early teenage daughters. The daughters sometimes relish the power that this gives them in the relationship and set out to exploit it to their own social, sexual and material advantage — in this case to the disadvantage of both an over-anxious mother and a frantic father.

Chapter 9
Becoming a professional

The test of our progress is not whether we add more to the abundance of those who have much; it is whether we provide enough for those who have too little. (F.D. Roosevelt, Second Inaugural Address.)

When approaching this chapter it is worth bearing in mind that literally anyone can set up as a counsellor or psychotherapist through an advertisement in the local paper, an entry in *Yellow Pages* and by putting a brass plate on the door. The only substantial inhibiting factor would probably be the difficulty in getting insurance cover as a protection from allegations of bad practice. I suspect a person setting up in such a manner would have no special anxiety in not being able to get cover and, indeed, may not have any or sufficient assets to be worth suing. You can't get blood from a stone!

Although now there is a registration body for counsellors, the British Association for Counselling, and for psychotherapists the United Kingdom Council for Psychotherapy, these are voluntary bodies and no counsellor or therapist can be required to join and submit themselves to the conditions of registration of either body before setting up in practice. The reader may feel that this is a disgraceful situation but there are perfectly good arguments against compulsory registration, not the least being the difficulty of defining what counselling and psychotherapy actually are and what practitioners actually do. I remember discussing the problem with an 'alternative therapist' who I regard as a capable and 'safe' therapist and he said, 'Well, if they bring in compulsory registration for psychotherapists I shall simply change my title'. I know he would and he has my sympathy. Another more esoteric objection is that both counselling and psychotherapy are emerging, developing and to some extent converging. Jeremy Holmes (1997) notes the tendency of one-time rival therapies to come together as therapeutic ways of working with those experiencing mental distress and for those searching for freedom through a clearer view of themselves. The situation is dynamic and it would be dangerous to offer the Holy Grail of therapeutic knowledge into the keeping of institutional bodies who would almost certainly protect their possession by restriction and regulation. Nothing is more deadening and threatening to new discovery and innovation. Imagine what would have happened if the investigations of Freud, Jung, Adler, Reich, Fromm and all the rest of those extraordinary early twentieth-century explorers of the human psyche, if they had been prohibited by state or medical restriction and registration. It was difficult enough struggling against the prejudices of the medical hierarchy of the time, which certainly would have prohibited their activities given half a chance. To explore this idea further it is worth reading Thomas Szasz, especially his article in the spring edition (1997) of the *British Journal of Psychotherapy*, in which he closely examines the nature of the relationship between therapist and client.

Although there is no legal requirement for a psychotherapist to be registered with an accrediting institute, nevertheless it is becoming clear that the movement in that direction is well under way and will, in all probability, come about some time in the fairly near future whether we like it or not. The question of legal registration in the future is far from clear. So the message is, register with an institute. Most institutes have demanding requirements for registration as a practising psychotherapist and an applicant may need to extend his/her training to meet their demands. It is to be hoped that full membership of the chosen institute will bring with it registration with the United Kingdom Council for Psychotherapy. For counsellors it is a rather different situation. The training bodies are not in themselves qualifying bodies and the British Association for Counselling lays down the qualifying conditions for professional counsellors. Alongside the question of professional recognition comes the requirement to be accountable.

Most registering institutes have a complaints procedure and an ethical code of practice and the members are reminded from time to time of the requirements of the institute in that respect. But, and it is a big but, clients will sometimes make claims against a therapist for financial damages that they perceive to arise out of malpractice. This may not enter the field of ethics but centre upon what is perceived as inadequate or unprofessional practice which, it is alleged, gives rise to damage and suffering. So the wise therapist and counsellor needs to be provided with some protection in this respect. In fact it is a must to find an insurer who will offer protection and legal advice. At one time this was very difficult but now virtually all professional bodies will put the therapist in touch with a reputable insurer. The PPS —The Psychologist's Protection Society — offers good insurance cover together with a legal advice service at very reasonable charges. Their cover also includes a useful public liability feature. The only alternative is to own nothing so that you are not worth suing. A gloomy lawyer gave me that advice many years ago. I did not follow it!

However, the best protection from malpractice accusations is to be a good practitioner, and that means always thinking through any consequences of your behaviour within your practice. There is an increasing awareness and concern about sexual activity in therapy. It appears that an increasing number of therapists are becoming sexually involved with patients. There is even a kind of tolerance of stories of therapists in the past taking patients as lovers or mistresses. Carl Jung is an example of the seducing therapist and is widely referred to in this respect, sometimes with humour and sometimes not. Although Freud broke many of his own rules he was honourably free of this misdemeanour. The rule is quite simple: no one should have any sexual relationship with a client, in no matter what guise, whilst the client is in therapy. I had a woman client many years ago who had been approached by an alternative therapist to have sexual intercourse with him as part of the loving, concerned aspect of therapy he offered. He assured my client that his wife knew about the offer and approved of it. My client refused but admitted to me that she had been tempted. She had experienced much confusion and anxiety concerning the possibility that she might be a lesbian and half thought that sex with this man would cure her of what she saw as the dreaded possibility of being homosexual. She went on to have a vigorous sexual relationship with a male work colleague to test her disposition, without much success. My view was that her emotional and sexual orientation was towards women. Her experiments with men seemed largely defensive. There are naturally moments of sexual frisson in the therapeutic relationship and to deny them is to be foolish and at risk in the therapeutic alliance. A recent trainee therapist suggested that he should not work with an attractive 25-year-old women because he felt the stirring of an erection in her presence. My feeling was that he was not at risk because he recognized and spoke openly about the issue with me. As a result he could exercise a decent inhibition of his desire and examine it with some curiosity in a safe supervisory situation.

There are of course many other areas of malpractice, often relating to money, wills, gifts and presents of all kinds. I knew a doctor/therapist who accepted a new motor car as a gift from grateful elderly women patients every year or so, in order that he could continue to visit and treat them at their homes without difficulty. Some years ago a young woman client gave me an expensive parting present. I was taken by surprise at the time and felt uneasy; I still do. Refusing it in the final moments of the last session of therapy seemed, at the time, both ungracious and impossible. I imagine a psychoanalyst would have declared the therapy incomplete and attributed the present to unresolved transference. And that might well have been the case. I now try to anticipate such gestures and tactfully inhibit them. I do sometimes receive presents of a more modest kind.

Sometimes, malpractice is not directly experienced by the client. In my view malpractice may take the form of abusive discussion between counsellors or therapists; the client is disparaged or simply objectified in terms of symptoms. This brings the profession into disrepute. A test is for the therapist to enter into the position of the client and speculate about the feelings that would arise in oneself in becoming the subject of such verbal abuse. Nevertheless, false accusations may well occur and the therapist or counsellor, no matter how scrupulous, could find him/herself at the receiving end of legal intimidation or action. An example would be where a client overdoses, resulting in brain damage with all its consequences. Concerned relatives, who may have treated therapy with scepticism, might feel angry towards the man's therapist and decide that there is a case of negligence to be pursued. The message is clear: get insured.

Being professional is to be well informed and authoritative. When I first came to live in Manchester some seven years ago I was dismayed to find that the library book request inter-library loan service had been suspended. The self-employed counsellor or therapist who has no access to a university library faces a considerable dilemma in keeping up to date with the constantly presented new writing in the field of psychotherapy and counselling. Books are very expensive and textbooks, with limited sale potential, particularly so. It is possible to get tax relief on the money spent on books but the reality is that most self-employed therapists and counsellors can only afford so many each year. One way out of this problem is to use the local library loan and inter-library loan service. After about a year the Manchester system got started again and with careful advanced planning I find I can get most books I want and need to read. It takes about three weeks to get a book and the cost is small.

If you are a keen and quick reader who likes to write and if you have sufficient self-confidence you could try your hand at writing reviews. The reward is to get your review copy free and gradually your personal library of hardback books builds up very satisfactorily. You also get the benefit of the contents of the book. A good starting place is within your own institute, where the institute publishes a journal. Usually editors are hungry for material and they often have a stack of books sent to them for review. All this takes time but at least the costs are negligible. There is a similar problem with the endlessly proliferating journals that keep coming onto the market. Most of them have some legitimacy but there is a considerable overlap, and sorting out the relevant journal that you need to read, to refresh your learning and to keep you in touch with contemporary developments is not easy. Again, if you have reading and borrowing status with your local university, then that is a fortunate circumstance; if not then a sympathetic local library will sometimes help in this respect, but in our present cost-conscious social milieu the chances are pretty slim.

You may decide that working through another aspect of therapy or counselling interests you. For years I have been involved in training psychotherapists, either in this country or abroad, sometimes in the theory and practice of analytic therapy and sometimes in creative therapies. Quite by chance I came into a professional working relationship with a highly competent and skilful Polish psychotherapist/clinical psychologist. We became good friends and after he returned to Poland I kept up personal and professional contacts with him. Poland was then a Communist state under the control of Marshal Jarulselski. Personal contact with George was relatively easy and I had a strong desire to go to Poland and do some workshops with him; he was pioneering psychotherapeutic approaches within the Polish NHS. To cut a long story short we overcame a number of difficulties and I made a number of visits to Warsaw and Cracow to carry out short training programmes, mainly in the area of group psychotherapy. I found these visits exciting and satisfying, a creative stimulating alternative to my more conservative regime of work in the UK.

The visits eventually led to invitations to visit Budapest in Hungary and St Petersburg in what was then the USSR. I approached work in Russia with some care and discrimination, being all too well aware of the way the mental hospitals had detained and abused political dissenters. Although these were work visits the conditions were so novel that I came to regard them as recreational visits. This was reinforced by the fact that my wife accompanied me on the trips abroad. When we stayed in Russia for some weeks she played the role of minder and housekeeper. In addition she had her own professional interests as a writer to pursue. We rented a flat through personal contacts. This was strictly speaking not legal; it added an extra frisson to the adventure of working in Russia. Getting food was a daily preoccupation. My wife came to enjoy the challenge. Like virtually all Russians I carried a plastic bag in my briefcase in case I saw a luxury item on a stall or in a shop: potatoes. I also viewed every queue with intense interest. The local traders soon came to recognize the 'mad' English people and treated us with consideration, often giving us a little priority to make up for our problem with the language. At a lighter level we used to say that we were the generation that could survive in the Russia of shortages and officious bureaucracy. We were the generation of the Second World War, when everyone was severely rationed and every aspect of life was controlled. Obviously, to coin a well-used cliché, 'one man's meat is another man's poison'. I found these adventures in Eastern Europe and Russia nurturing and refreshing. The narcissistic element in my personality was rewarded. It was nice to be made much of, to be valued, being viewed as a novel, somewhat exotic figure by the participants in these training workshops. Maybe I was something of a prophet without honour in his own country enjoying celebration in foreign parts. Therapists and counsellors would be wise to find their own outlet for that creative aspect of themselves, wherever it rests.

I have referred to the many seminars, workshops and conferences organized every year that attract us. There is a kind of roundabout of 'star' performers that most of us would like to meet and engage with in some kind of learning context but the cost of such events continues to spiral. For the professional therapist and counsellor working for the NHS or some other voluntary organization there is usually training money available in the budget that can be drawn on to subsidize further training. The money has shrunk over the years but as far as the self-employed therapist is concerned it has never existed. Again, the taxman will usually accept these costs as legitimate expenses, so that is some comfort, but tax relief is only as significant as the amount of money you earn. The advantages of going to workshops and conferences are pretty obvious. We all need to replenish our stocks of knowledge and skill; indeed it is expected of the professional therapist and counsellor that he/she is and remains well informed and knowledgeable.

Meeting colleagues on a regular basis is of great help to a psychotherapist working alone, perhaps at home. It can be a lonely life. In psychoanalysis it is suggested that the therapist is working at an emotional deficit, and that is certainly true for many psychotherapists working as standalone practitioners. I mentioned earlier belonging to a Regional Psychotherapy Association, which I find nourishing at both a professional and personal level. We do not gossip about patients, although we are quite an amusing group of people. We do discuss psychotherapy issues with some seriousness as well as share more personal experiences in both a concerned and entertaining way. Our membership is cosmopolitan and we encompass a range of therapists and counsellors working in different styles and orientations. This is healthy. The contrasts between us inform and educate and inspire us to regard each other with curiosity, interest and respect.

Personal interests beyond psychotherapy are a must if the therapist is going to stay healthy in a social as well as psychological way. I like to sing and belong to a community choir, I enjoy novels, keep up with the latest films and go regularly to concerts, dance and theatre. Living in Manchester makes all this possible and living with a wife who shares all these interests is a great advantage. But this is no prescription for a healthy life. Each individual must chart a path of self-expression and development. The point is to engage with those aspects of your personality that need creative expression, whether it be socializing, walking, gardening, attending further education classes, or whatever. No pursuit is in itself necessarily superior to another; the point is to consciously aim to live as good a life as possible and to avoid living a professional life that deprives rather than fulfils. For the psychotherapist and counsellor this is not altogether easily achieved; a life trying to help others fulfil personal needs, overcoming neurotic distortions, can be a life that marginalizes the therapist's own personal development. It may leave us working at an emotional and social deficit.

More and more counsellors and therapists are entering public service through various agencies. Talking to a newly qualified psychotherapist, I found myself reassuring her about her position as a psychotherapist within a hospital setting. Dealing with a team of about ten psychiatrists and dozens of nurses and other health auxiliaries, as well as social and community workers, she felt her professional identity was often threatened and her position of clinical independence, practice and judgement challenged by the customary ways of working in the hospital. This was my experience too when working sessionally in a large NHS mental hospital and even after a dozen years of service it remained a continuing presence in my professional life. My response was to establish my professionalism in a number of ways. I asserted it in the practice of therapy, which simply meant I upheld the principles and practice of psychotherapy in circumstances that invited me to abandon, at least in part, some ways of working and behaving that I regarded as central to my professionalism. Not least among these pressures was the pressure to dehumanize my patients by referring to them symptomatically rather than by their proper names, as discussed in an earlier chapter. A simple illustration was when staff talked of him or her as a category rather than a person: in terms of being a manic depressive or schizophrenic, as if these clinical terms were enough to account for the person. I would insist upon a proper recognition of the person concerned by using the woman or man's title and full name. This may sound like a 'holier than thou stance'. I am sure some people thought me too rigid and unbending in the matter of identifying patients, in either their presence or absence. Even the casual use of Christian names can reduce and undermine the dignity of patients in institutional settings. As one patient said to me, 'If another person calls me "love" I shall scream'.

In the hospital there was a need constantly to assert proper clinical boundaries. This could simply be by refusing porters a right of entry into a room where group therapy was taking place. Even establishing a therapy room and equipping it sympathetically and exclusively is often a major difficulty, or for that matter always seeking the permission of patients when other clinicians wanted to visit and observe work in practice. There are many other examples. Perhaps one of the most important boundaries was keeping to the timing of organized appointments and refusing to let them be marginalized by other demands. The essence of professionalism is the insistence on certain valued forms of conduct. These will vary from one profession to another but the practice of counselling and psychotherapy not being primarily of a medical character often promotes challenge in institutions immersed in a nursing or medical culture.

The other way of maintaining a position of psychotherapeutic professionalism was simply to assert it in everyday conversations and encounters. In one hospital unit where I worked I noticed I was never introduced to visitors by title, e.g. 'Don the psychotherapist'. A vague, non-specific introduction was used by the charge nurse along the following lines: 'Oh this is Don, he comes in once a week and works with us'. For a long time I tolerated this and then decided there was an underground message of professional rivalry and envy at work So at the next opportunity I jumped in with my own introduction before she could account for me in the usual ambiguous way. As the visitor approached me I would stick out my hand for a handshake and say, 'I'm Don Feasey, I work here as a non-medical psychotherapist'. And of course the term 'non-medical' conveys a good deal, it is a simple phrase containing many levels of meaning. If the nursing staff did not wish to identify me it was not simply because they resented my role in the unit, or the fact that on an hourly basis I was better paid than they were, or undertook duties they were not entrusted with, or would not have sought to perform. Rather their reluctance was based on genuine confusion about what precisely is the medical aspect of psychotherapy. Paradoxically it appears that the best protection for a lay therapist or counsellor, in a hospital or clinic setting, is patronage by a consultant psychiatrist or consultant clinical psychologist. For most therapists and counsellors in the community this issue is probably not a vital one but the counsellor or therapist working in a clinical setting, as more and more do, will quickly find it is a matter that is not easily answered.

The group that is probably most engaged with this issue is those counsellors who work doing sessions in GP practices. As yet there are no established protocols governing the work of counsellors in GP practices. The majority of counsellors, who are registered with the British Association for Counselling (BAC), will have to maintain the professional standards and ethics advanced by that body. But the BAC is not a trade union or negotiating body dealing with pay and conditions of work and it seems, from my personal enquiries, that many counsellors in GP practices are badly paid and lacking in professional support from their employers. The most a counsellor can do in such a situation is to uphold a professional position.

First and foremost it is essential to establish the basic conditions for good counselling: A secure and pleasant counselling room needs to be obtained and respect given to the counsellor's use of it, where use is shared. A proper appointments system needs to be in place with sufficient time allocated for each patient, which is confidential and respectful. A simple infrastructure of secretarial support is necessary and it is useful for the counsellor to have proper access to the doctors in the practice when consultation is needed. This must always be with the agreement of the patient. Similarly, the counsellor needs to be present at staff meetings where both clinical and administrative decisions are made which may well impinge on his/her practice as a counsellor. It seems likely that eventually the *ad hoc* arrangements that counsellors now experience, even suffer, in their employment by GPs will give place to a properly organized and coherent professional system but, until then, the present generation of counsellors need to fend for themselves. This is very important because they are laying down the basic conditions upon which future generations of counsellors will build.

I have been writing as if counsellors and psychotherapists are born rather than made. But of course most of them come to counselling or therapy from earlier experiences of training and work with people. Many come from nursing, medicine, teaching and social work backgrounds. A few have trained as psychologists and have worked either in education, industry or within a clinical setting. I came from a primary training in youth and community work followed by lecturing in vocational higher education. Most of us have already shown our commitment to working in some sort of human enterprise concerned with growth, development and reparation. So when we come to our therapy or counselling training we are bringing with us considerable personal baggage. Dealing with this baggage, as I call it, is sometimes painful. A trainee client recently complained of the infantalization that took place in training, where his previous experience as a senior academic in a university was completely ignored. Often trainees are treated as blank sheets of paper upon which the theory and practice of counselling and therapy are written during their training. Some of the previous experience of a trainee is very useful but some of it is a hindrance. Most of us introject aspects of our previous working life that are not appropriate to the practice of therapy or counselling. For example, we may have been in a work culture where it is quite usual to give advice or to share everyday experiences with students, children or clients. For the most part, to do so in counselling or therapy is quite inappropriate, although clients may well look to us for a little wisdom. This background needs recognition and acknowledgement, especially through supervision, in order that the creative and positive elements of the trainee's professional past are valued and inappropriate elements consciously put aside, not as valueless but as not applicable in the field of counselling or psychotherapy.

Finally, let me consider the contentious issue of the known effectiveness of psychotherapy and counselling. In this age of 'tactics', 'strategies' and 'outcomes', where attempts are made to quantify and measure virtually all aspects of human behaviour, it is inevitable that some people will look for verifiable evidence that psychotherapy and counselling are effective interventions in the experience of emotional and mental disorder. Research material is thin on the ground and some of it not entirely convincing. A sharp punchy article in *Changes* (1992) by David Smail attacks the idea that therapy can bring about significant change in the personality. He seems to be saying we are what we are and that all the talking in the world is not going to change us in any significant way. Although admitting that human beings can change for the better, whatever that may mean, he argues that when change occurs we do not usually understand the process, although we may attribute it to counselling or psychotherapy. Oddly enough, Jeffrey Masson (1992), in one of his most condemning attacks on psychoanalytic psychotherapy, hardly bothers to examine its curative efficacy. Indeed, despite his massive disillusion with the current psychoanalytical world, especially the 'British School', he still gives Freud much credit and states: 'even if all of Freud's ideas were not right, the method — patiently, humbly listening to another person tell his or her life story — was correct and could be beneficial'.

It is not for me here to discuss the most recent discourses in the area of quantitative and qualitative research but readers who are interested could benefit from reading the special issue of *Changes* (1996), which examines the discussion in some detail. Certainly it is true that counselling and psychotherapy do not emerge as being especially effective when judged through a quantitive approach. However, I was concerned with a research project conducted in association with an NHS psychotherapy unit. The proposition was that patients who had gone through the programme would show benefit after discharge from the unit. This was measured in terms that reflected Freud's view that the basic life task is to love and to work. This proposition was examined against the individual situations of the discharged patients at the time of leaving and in consequent follow-up interviews. The results, overall, were satisfactory and rewarding to the therapists and the group analytic form of the therapy. To my mind, however, a more objective form of measurement was even more impressive. An enquiry was mounted to find out whether discharged patients went back to their GP complaining of the problems that had been encountered before the therapy. Most of the patients had not been the subject of further psychiatric assessment and treatment. This was compared with a group of patients who had not received psychotherapeutic treatment, to the advantage of the treated group members. This is described in detail by Dr B. Dick in *The Evolution of Group Analysis* (Pines, 1983).

Certainly professional therapists and counsellors will attribute effectiveness and value to the practice of therapy and counselling, as a way of expressing confidence in themselves and their work. Who can blame them? Whilst there is evidence that we can gain more insight into ourselves through counselling and therapy, the evidence that we act to change ourselves on the basis of that insight is nowhere near as certain. Any therapist, of whatever orientation, must address this issue, if only privately in the 'wee small hours'. My position is quite clear to me. I look for change in the client in the relationship with me and how it relates to evidence of change in his/her network of relationships outside the therapy room. I am not looking for evidence of massive change in the basic personality of my client, rather I am concerned to detect how the client manages the complexities of human relationships during therapy and whether he/she appears to achieve better outcomes for him/herself and those around him/her. In some of the cases I have presented in this book I think it is obvious that the clients concerned had made adjustments in their lives that might be described as healthy ones, challenging repetitive patterns of the past and admitting insight into the conduct of their relationships with those around them in an active and creative way.

In conclusion, I think it bears repetition to state that the art of counselling and psychotherapy lies in the unique quality of the relationship that is offered to those who seek to use the service, either as clients or therapists. I am encouraged by the manner in which counselling, in one of its most important aspects, is now moving more and more towards understanding that the *use* of the relationship between counsellor and client is the essence of the counselling dialogue. This is sometimes called psychodynamic counselling. Similarly it is obvious that the analytic approach used in the training of many psychotherapists now places more emphasis on objective aspects of the therapeutic alliance. As a consequence clients are given more empowerment, are offered more information and explanation of the forms of therapy and are properly valued for their gender, race and culture. The empathetic qualities of the counselling world are offered, not replacing but complementing the emphasis on the fantasies of the so-called transference relationship.

The words I am using such as empowerment, empathy, transference, fantasy, counselling and analysis are only means of describing a relationship between people. Over the years I know I have gained much from my training and practice as a psychotherapist. This knowledge gives me strength to go on working with clients and colleagues in the awareness that it is the quality of the relationship with human beings that determines personal happiness and shapes our destiny. My beginnings as a psychoanalytic psychotherapist started from deeply felt humanistic beliefs. My development as a human being and therapist has proceeded from that philosophical position, and if there has been a change it is in the degree of awareness and understanding I have managed to acquire of my philosophy. I still feel it deeply but now I understand it more clearly.

References

Brenner C (1957) Psychoanalysis. New York: Anchor.

Breuer J, Freud S (1974) Studies on Hysteria. London: Pelican.

Changes (1996) Special Issue, 14(3).

Clark S (1967) What Freud Really Said. London: Pelican.

Coltart N (1993) How to Survive as a Psychotherapist. London: Sheldon Press.

Dick B (1983) In Pines M (Ed.) Evolution of Group Analysis. London: Tavistock.

Dryden W (Ed.) (1984) Individual Psychotherapy in Britain. London: Harper & Row.

Feasey D (1996) The return of the repressed. British Journal of Psychodrama and Sociodrama 11 (1 and 2).

Feasey D (1997) The experience of supervision. Changes 15(1).

Feasey D (1998) Will it or won't it work? Changes 16(2).

Freud S (1976) The Interpretation of Dreams. London: Pelican,Vol. 4.

Freud S (1913/1966) On Beginning the Treatment, Standard Edition. London: Hogarth Press.

Freud S (1974) The Question of Lay Analysis. London: Pelican, Vol. 15.

Freud S (1974) Collected Works. London: Pelican.

Freud S (1975) Introductory Lectures in Psychoanalysis. London: Pelican.

Freud S, Breuer J (1974) Studies on Hysteria. London: Pelican, Vol. 3.

Foulkes SH, Anthony EJ (1973) Group Psychotherapy. London: Pelican.

Fromm-Reichmann F (1950) Principles of Intensive Psychotherapy. Chicago: Chicago University Press.

Frosh S (1992) Sexual Differences: Masculinity and Psychoanalysis. London: Routledge.

Gray A (1994) Introduction to the Therapeutic Frame. London: Routledge.

Guthrie E, Moore J, Barker H, Margison F, McGrath G (1998) Clinical paper: Brief psychodynamic intervention. British Journal of Psychotherapy 15(2).

Holmes J (1997) The Future of Counselling. London: Sage.

Jones E (1974) Sigmund Freud. Life and Work. London: Pelican.

Laing RD (1960) The Divided Self. Harmondsworth: Penguin.

Malcolm J (1982) Psychoanalysis: The Impossible Profession. London: Pan Books.

Masson J (1992) Final Analysis. London: Fontana.

Pepper FS (Ed. Comp.) (1985) 20th Century Quotations. London: Sphere.

Pines M (Ed.) (1983) The Evolution of Group Analysis. London: Routledge & Kegan Paul.

Polden J (1998) Published and be damned. British Journal of Psychotherapy 15(2).

Prodgers A (1991) On Hating the Patient. British Journal of Psychotherapy 8.

Rogers C (1971) On Becoming a Person. London: Constable.

Smail D (1992) Psychotherapeutic theory and wishful thinking. Changes 10(4).

Szasz T (1998) Discretion as power. British Journal of Psychotherapy 15(2).

Storr (1979) The Art of Psychotherapy. London: Secker & Warburg.

Tillett R (1998) Therapeutic aggression. British Journal of Psychotherapy 15(3).

Venier K (1998) Confidentiality and psychotherapy. British Journal of Psychotherapy15(2).

Winnicott WD (1958) Collected Papers. London: Tavistock.

Index